PIERRE-JULIEN EYMARD

THE PRIEST OF THE EUCHARIST

Pierre-Julien Eymard
The Priest of the Eucharist

Founder of the
Fathers of the Blessed Sacrament
and of the
Sister-Servants of the Blessed Sacrament

by
Albert Tesnière, s s s

THE CENACLE PRESS
AT SILVERSTREAM PRIORY

This edition is based on the 1926 printing by The Sentinel Press under the title *Blessed Peter Julian Eymard: The Priest of the Eucharist*.

Design of this edition © 2023 Silverstream Priory.
The text of the original edition is in the public domain.

All reservable rights reserved for the new material of this edition.
No part of the new material of this edition may be reproduced or transmitted, in any form or by any means, without permission.

Nihil Obstat
Eugène Couet, sss
Superior Generalis

Nihil Obstat
Arthur J. Scanlan, std
Censor Librorum

Imprimatur
✠ Patrick Cardinal Hayes
Archiepiscopus Neo Eboracensis

New York
31 January 1926

The Cenacle Press at Silverstream Priory
Silverstream Priory
Stamullen, County Meath, K32 T189, Ireland
www.cenaclepress.com

ISBN 978-1-915544-78-0

Book design by Kenneth Lieblich
Cover design by Silverstream Priory

CONTENTS

	Foreword	vii
I	Early Days—He Enters the Priesthood	1
II	His Life as a Pastor	7
III	His Religious Life—He is Drawn to the Eucharist	11
IV	His Life Work Revealed	17
V	Foundation of the Congregation of the Blessed Sacrament	25
VI	Life of the Fathers of the Blessed Sacrament	31
VII	His Eucharistic Preaching	41
VIII	Eucharistic Apostolate	45
IX	The Priests' Eucharistic League	51
X	The People's Eucharistic League	53
XI	The Sister-Servants of the Blessed Sacrament—The Cenacle	63
XII	Personal Sanctification	67
XIII	Modesty, Humility and Kindness	71
XIV	Trials	75
XV	Our Lady of the Most Blessed Sacrament	81
XVI	Death of Blessed Eymard	85
XVII	The Process of Beatification	91
XVIII	The Two Miracles—The Beatification	95

FOREWORD

This little volume was published in French in 1870, two years after the death of Pierre-Julien Eymard, under the title of "The Priest of the Eucharist."

The author had been admitted into the Congregation of the Blessed Sacrament, at the age of eighteen, by the Founder himself; he therefore knew him most intimately. He had also the sad satisfaction, when he hurried to his death bed, of rendering him a final testimony of filial devotion.

After publishing, under the title of "The Divine Eucharist," several volumes taken from the manuscripts and sermons of Blessed Eymard, which today have a wide circulation in several languages, he further developed his spiritual father's teaching and preserved its spirit. At the same time he contributed greatly to the work of the Congregation of the Priests of the Blessed Sacrament, and to the definite organization of the Sisters Servants of the Blessed Sacrament.

He died in Paris in 1909, one year after having had the consolation of seeing the introduction of the Cause of Beatification of his revered father, whose likeness he had portrayed so faithfully, and whose spiritual heritage he had so carefully transmitted.

We have inserted here and there some facts as stated by witnesses who testified during the Apostolic processes, as the author would certainly have added them to his text, had it been possible for him to work at the final preparations of the Cause. He would have worked hard at this task, as was characteristic of him, and his joy would have known no bounds had he been present in St Peter's on July 12, 1925, the day of the Beatification.

THE POSTULATOR OF THE CAUSE

I

HIS BIRTH — EARLY DAYS — HE ENTERS THE PRIESTHOOD

"How the good God has deigned to love me! He led me by the hand to the Society of the Blessed Sacrament. All His graces have been means of preparation for this end; and the Eucharist has been the dominant thought of my life. The Blessed Virgin kept alive this feeling in my heart; it is she who first led me to my Eucharistic Lord."

Such were the words of that Priest of the Eucharist whom we wish to make known to our readers. Born at La Mure d'Isère, on February 4, 1811, of a thoroughly Christian father and a mother whose piety was as enlightened as it was fervent, the boy received the next day, at the baptismal font, the names of Pierre-Julien. He was still at the breast when his mother took him with her to church. She was very fond of assisting at Benediction, and perhaps the first intelligent looks of the babe were directed towards the monstrance. When he could hardly toddle, he would always try and follow his mother in her daily visit to the Blessed Sacrament; and people used to remark that the child never fidgeted or seemed weary of it like other children, and never begged to go out, however long might be his mother's prayers in the church.

His sister, who was ten years older than himself, and who became as his second mother, went frequently to Holy Communion. One day, when little Peter was four or five years old, he said to her:

"You are very happy to be allowed to go to Communion so often. Do offer it some day for me."

"For you!" she replied, much surprised. "But what do you know about it? What do you want me to ask for you?"

Peter answered:

"Ask Our Lord to make me very good and gentle and pure, so that I may be a priest some day."

To become a priest—that was, even at such a tender age, the one ambition of this child of predilection. We may imagine how his sister, who loved him passionately, kept these words in her heart.

Another instance proved how early the child had understood the two principal duties of piety towards the God hidden in the Tabernacle—*i.e.,* to keep Him company, and thus honor His Presence amongst us; and to unite oneself to that great Sacrifice of reparation for the salvation of men.

On one occasion the child was missing, and that for several hours. At last, he was discovered kneeling on a little stool, which he had dragged close to the high altar of the parish church, with his hands clasped, and his eyes fixed upon the Tabernacle.

"What are you about?" exclaimed his mother.

"I am close to Jesus, and listening to Him," replied the child.

He was "listening";—the part of Mary at Nazareth and at Bethany; the "better" part, as declared by Our Lord Himself.

His little heart was already inflamed as it were, with the love of God. One day he placed a cord around his neck, took off his shoes, and, fancying he was quite alone in the church, came with a candle in his hand to make amends to the Prisoner of Love. He was surprised in the act, and laughed at for his folly. But Our Lord is said to hunger and thirst for souls thus pure and innocent; and the child preserved during his whole life the untarnished brightness of his baptismal robe. Long before his first Communion he begged to go to confession, which was generally refused, as he was considered too young. But sometimes he would steal off with a boy older than himself to a priest in a village two leagues from La Mure, and there seek the tribunal of penance.

"How glad I am!" he exclaimed one day, on coming back from this excursion. "How happy I feel! I am pure now!"

One day he exclaimed, with a touching simplicity: "I committed many sins in my childhood. Once I stole a soldier's plume from a shop; but repentance followed quickly, and I ran and threw it back again."

To his confession he added vigorous penances, putting boards into his bed, and fasting often. Even that did not satisfy his zeal, though it was too much for his weak little stomach. Towards eleven o'clock, when he felt hunger too keenly, he would run to the church, so as to cheat himself by this innocent device.

At last came the happy moment of his first Communion. We only know of one little word which passed between Our Lord and His young servant in that first moment of union:

"When I felt Jesus in my breast I exclaimed, *'I will be a priest; I promise it to Thee.'*"

Thirty years later the remembrance of this day brought tears to the good Father Eymard.

"Oh, what graces Our Lord gave me at the moment of my first Communion!" he one day said to his students. "Yes, I feel and believe that my conversion was then sincere and perfect."

That same year he enlisted himself in the Confraternity of the Sacred Heart, which he always called "his great safeguard."

His first Communion awoke in his heart the most earnest desire to renew it frequently. He begged and entreated leave for this in vain for a long while. At last, after a pilgrimage which he made, at thirteen, to Notre-Dame du Laus, a venerable missionary gave him permission to go to Communion every week. As he said, "Mary thus gave me Jesus."

But the thought of the priesthood was the absorbing one in the boy's heart. It needed a solid and real vocation to triumph over the obstacles which he had to encounter. His father positively refused him leave to study. A clever cutler himself, and a good mechanician, he had invented a new system of machinery for an oil-press, which was a great success. Naturally proud of his invention, he wanted to interest his son in it likewise. The boy, placing himself under the protection of Our Lady, carried on his studies in secret. Out of his slender allowance he contrived to buy some Latin books second-hand, and arrived, by dint of perseverance, at mastering the rudiments of the language.

"In order to get my exercises corrected," he writes, "I used to ask the charitable help of the young seminarists who were spending their holidays at La Mure; but sometimes they would drive me away, because they said I smelt of oil."

But time went on, and he was seventeen. A zealous missionary of the Oblates of Mary, who had watched the boy's conduct and knew the secret of his studies, at last obtained his father's consent—though with great difficulty—to his following his vocation.

Thanks to him, Pierre-Julien entered the novitiate at Marseille. But just when he thought his difficulties were over, and his career certain, a dangerous illness forced him to return home after only ten months' study. He had scarcely recovered, when he was called to his father's death bed. Being afterwards placed as sacristan in a church at Grenoble, he heard suddenly that his mother was no more. Then, throwing himself at the feet of Mary, and shedding torrents of tears, he took her for his mother, conjuring her to bring about some means of enabling him to follow his vocation.

This prayer was heard. His faith and patience had been sufficiently tried; and in a most unexpected manner, he suddenly found the doors of the Great Seminary at Grenoble opened to him. He remained there three years, and by his extraordinary industry very soon made up for the time he had previously lost. We have an eye-witness of his behavior during his college life in one of his fellow-students, who writes as follows:

"The simple and earnest piety of Peter Eymard seemed to us to expand more and more at the Grand Seminary, and his love of God increased day by day. His greatest pleasure—for which we had every facility in the college—was to visit Jesus very often in the Blessed Sacrament."

Among his "resolutions" during the retreat of that first year we find this note: "I feel that I do not show enough love to Jesus in the Blessed Sacrament. I mean that in my devotions before the Tabernacle I think too much, and do not pray enough. I will try and amend this in future."

Already Our Lord would fill his heart and be his only book.

His fellow-student's letter goes on to say:

"Eymard was presented before any of the others for tonsure and minor orders, which proved what our superiors thought, not only of his progress in learning but of his virtue and wisdom. He was, in fact, a subject of edification to us all. During the vacations, he would gather together all the children he could find in the villages, and teach them little ways of faith and piety by which he gave vent to his fervent zeal and love of souls. But when it came to his preparation for receiving the priesthood, it is impossible to describe how he behaved. God alone has his secret. All I can say is, that it was enough for us ordinary mortals to watch him, not only during his studies, but during recreation and especially in church, to feel ourselves impelled to greater fervor and love."

He went into retreat before his ordination on July 15, 1834. He examined his past life, reckoning up his faults as a severe judge, and resolving "to implore of God without ceasing a greater horror of venial sins, with the gift of tears to weep for those already committed." He dwelt especially on the most terrible realities, the certainty of judgment and of hell. "There is a hell," he writes. "Many priests are in it. Shall I be one of that number? Yes, if I am such a coward in prayer, in humility, in mortification, in love of humiliations. Yes, if I deny God by not daring on all occasions to confess Him."

"Implacable war against my pride," he writes, in large letters. "To begin at once to root it out."

Then, thinking with terror of the great action he was about to perform, he adds "This, my first Mass, may be my last. Let me be ready to die after having said it."

Thus, filled with a sense of his own nothingness, young Eymard received holy orders, and was ordained priest. It was on July 20, 1834. Directly after, without saying a word to his sister, or to anyone else, he fled to a pious solitude dedicated to Our Lady, and after a day of solemn preparation, recollection, and solitude, celebrated his first Mass.

Who shall speak of that hour, or of the delight of the servant and of the Master, reposing at his call in hands so pure and innocent? "It is good to hide the secret of the King" (Tob. xii. 7); but it is one which betrayed itself, by a strong visible emotion, when the Father went up to the altar, year by year, on the anniversary of his first Sacrifice.

II

HIS LIFE AS A PASTOR

From the moment he became a priest, Father Eymard seemed to live only for the Blessed Sacrament.

"More than two hours before his Mass," writes his sister, Mlle. Marianne, "my brother was unapproachable. He spent nearly as long a time afterwards in acts of praise and thanksgiving."

During the day he paid long visits to the Blessed Sacrament. To It he confided all his resolutions. Under the shadow of the Tabernacle he composed all his writings. The living presence of Our Lord was never absent from his thoughts. It was not an abstraction or a remembrance. "The Master" was there.

Next to his devotion to the Blessed Sacrament was his love of his neighbor. At Chatte first, and then at Monteynard, his whole life was devoted to his flock. His memory in both places is ever held in tenderest veneration. He took the most active part in all the interests of his parishioners, shared in their labors, suffered in their sorrows, rejoiced in their joys. He had learned a little medical skill, and practiced it freely, and with the greatest success, among the poor. Perhaps his prayers effected even more cures than his treatment. But the more miserable any one was, the more he preferred him. He would give away everything he had, down to his sister's clothes. "To keep the little money, which was absolutely necessary for our daily bread," she wrote, "I was obliged to hide it, and was only too happy when the ingenuity of his charity did not detect where I kept my hoard." One day, when her brother had given away their last franc, she exclaimed:

"But what on earth are we to eat?"

"Oh, there is some bread and cheese, isn't there, somewhere?" was his reply; and his poor housekeeper got no other satisfaction.

For five years he labored on in this parish, and learned all the difficulties and responsibilities of ministerial work. In a retreat given to the priests of the diocese in 1836, he seemed to hear Our Lord asking him from the Tabernacle, "Peter, lovest thou Me?" He replied, "Lord, I dare not say I love Thee; but I *will* love Thee." And he continued: "Oh, how happy should I be if I could be free from all other ties, with my heart chained to Jesus only! I will use every effort to divest my heart of all other interests, and to root out my besetting sin, which is always the same—pride. I will go before the Blessed Sacrament and sign this resolution with my blood"—which he did.

One word more about his parochial life, which was soon to cease. To insure the independence of his ministry, he never would accept the smallest present from any of his parishioners. He menaced those who insisted to cease all intercourse with them; so that they were obliged to yield and respect the fidelity of this true servant of Jesus Christ.

But one can understand how Our Lord, jealous of such a soul, had resolved to call him even more closely to Himself. He called him consequently to embrace the life of a religious. The Oblates of Mary had just been founded. Father Eymard was to share in the trials which are inseparable from all beginnings. Later on, he was to pass through similar trials, no longer as a follower, but as a leader; and remembering his past experience, he was never surprised at the storms which at one time threatened to overwhelm both himself and his work.

It was with very great difficulty that the venerable Archbishop of Grenoble could be persuaded to consent to his leaving his cure. Recognizing at last the Divine Will in the matter, Monsignor Philibert de Bruillard bore this witness to the merits of his faithful fellow-laborer:

"I think I cannot more strongly show my esteem for the Society of Mary than by giving them a priest like you."

He was then, as we have said, Curé of Monteynard. The day of his departure having arrived, he made up a little parcel of his linen and absolute necessaries, and went off secretly, without taking leave of anyone. Just as he had left the village he met his sister, who had been to Grenoble.

"Where are you going?" she exclaimed in dismay.

"I am going where the Will of God calls me. Adieu."

"Oh, my brother! my darling brother!" she cried, sobbing bitterly, "you cannot leave me like this. Stop, I implore you, if only for one day longer."

"No, my beloved sister," replied he, "it is impossible. Our Lord has called me today. Let me be faithful to His voice. Tomorrow it might be too late."

So, stifling the voice of nature, he left her and entered the novitiate. It was during the octave of the Assumption in the year 1839.

We have the notes of his retreats from year to year; some from month to month. They show the work of God in the soul of His faithful servant. But above all we see the strong leading of the Eucharistic grace. True, he has become a Marist. But in the designs of God, Our Blessed Lady leads him herself to the Tabernacle. Till the day of his death he would say, "Mary herself brought me to Our Lord."

III

HIS RELIGIOUS LIFE — HE IS DRAWN TO THE EUCHARIST

We will quote some of his notes, which have fallen into our hands, though intended solely for God and himself.

On entering the noviceship, August 28, 1839, he writes:

"I abandon myself with entire confidence in God until the hour of my death; and I feel I should die happy if I could only love Our Lord enough in the Sacrament of His love."

A few months later he writes: "My two favorite subjects of devotion are Jesus in the Blessed Sacrament, and Paradise, the vision of God. These two thoughts absorb my whole soul.

"The state to which Our Lord seems, as it were, to drive me, is one of intellectual death. I have no rest except in that state of nothingness.

"Our Lord has shown me that I must allow myself to be led or guided like a little child, who does the thing which is before him and nothing else. Thus I hope to arrive, by the sacrifice of my intellectual self, at a life of real death in Jesus Christ.

"When one realizes fully two things, one knows enough to become a great saint; that is, first, to own and love one's own nothingness; and, secondly, to throw oneself with entire confidence into the arms of God."

His novitiate over, he was appointed at once Director of the Little Seminary of Belley.

His notes generally begin thus: "Our Lord has shown me," "Our Lord made me understand." The God of the Eucharist was his real master. "I never had any other," he wrote once; "I believe I should have attached myself too much to anyone who had done me good. But, in reality, no human being ever pointed out to me what all along I was really seeking."

Speaking one day of the influence of the Eucharist on his childhood, he exclaimed, "Without the Blessed Sacrament I should certainly have been lost. At Fourvière Our Lord made me a loving reproach: 'What do you fear? Throw yourself into My arms.' I felt I could weep with love and confidence. For a long time Our Lord seems to pursue me. And I have always been clinging to some straw rather than throw myself into the abyss of love, where He is waiting for me. But this is over. At last, O my God, I am all Thine. My dominant thought is Jesus in the most Blessed Sacrament. My love is there." A little further on he writes: "If God did not wish me to be a saint He would not have created me; or He would have made me as the brute beasts. What strikes me most is the incredible state of humiliation and obedience in which Jesus places Himself in the Blessed Sacrament; that is certainly my great attraction." And again: "Our Saviour has made me see the urgent necessity of accusing myself of my faults as soon as committed, *i.e.,* of frequent confession, so as to be always in a state of grace." We might multiply extracts, but we have said enough to show what were the Father's feelings during the first five years of his religious life.

In 1845 he was appointed Provincial, which entailed far more serious and important duties. To prepare himself for them he takes the resolution "to empty himself completely, so that God might fill him with Himself; and to labor more earnestly at the annihilation of self, so that God should work great things in him according to His Will."

During the month of May in that year he received a special favor from Our Lord on the feast of Corpus Christi, which he thus describes:

"I had the great happiness this day of bearing the Blessed Sacrament in the procession at St Paul's, and my whole soul was filled with joy. I seemed penetrated with faith and love of the Sacred Host. The two hours it lasted seemed to me but so many minutes. I placed at the feet of the Blessed Sacrament the Church, France, the Society of Mary, myself, all that I hold most dear. My heart seemed as if swallowed up in His, and I longed to have all the hearts in the universe to give them to Jesus. Ever since this month began I have had an increased attraction towards the Blessed Eucharist. I have never felt it so strongly before. It seems to urge me on, whether in direction or in preaching, to bring all the world to love Jesus Christ, and to speak of Him alone in His Eucharistic love.... It is a settled thing. Henceforth this alone will be the object of all my prayers, all my wishes. I will take St Paul, that great Apostle of Our Lord, as my patron in this new apostolate; and my good Mother will initiate me into the great mystery of her Divine Son, and will personify it in me.... O my Lord, what a blessing if I deserved to hear from Thy mouth the words spoken to St Thomas, the Angelic Doctor, 'Thou hast spoken well of me, Peter.' Thou knowest, O God, my prayer during Thy triumphal procession. I repeated it again and again. Oh, the joy it gave me!"

Thus did this attraction increase day by day during the ten years which were yet to elapse before the foundation of the Society of the Blessed Sacrament. But at the same time he felt himself more and more drawn towards the hidden life, and an entire abandonment of his own will to that of Our Lord, which was to be his preparation for the final sacrifice.

He writes in September, 1845: "Our Lord fills me with love for a hidden life, and teaches me to avoid, as far as possible, making new acquaintances, or having much intercourse with people in the world. My great happiness would be to be able to say my Mass quite secretly, in an obscure little chapel, without a crowd." "Our Lord shows me special love in the Holy Eucharist. I will do everything to respond to it. But the principal virtue He requires of me is the abnegation of my own will. O my God, Thy will be done. Let me die to self, and my life henceforth be hidden in God with Jesus Christ in the Blessed Eucharist." Again: "Our Lord has made me clearly understand that to write or preach anything clearly and holily I must be inspired at His feet, that there alone my work would be blessed and become easy. I have resolved, therefore, never to write anything, or to make any plan, without having first meditated upon it before the Tabernacle and having submitted it to His approbation. After all, what does Our Lord require of me but the abnegation of my own will? that interior poverty which strips me of myself, of my mind, of my judgment, even of my heart."

In 1850, on New Year's Day, he writes: "To submit myself entirely to the Will of God, this shall be my *mot d'ordre* for the year. To abandon myself and my future entirely in His hands. With what Divine love has God ever led me where it was best for me, and always given me what suited best my state!"

He had founded that year a "Third Order" of Mary, which he had much at heart. Yet it met with endless contradictions. "God alone knows what the foundation of that Third Order cost me!" he wrote later.

In 1851 his Superior sent him to direct an important house of education at La Seyne-sur-Mer (Var). This is how he received the news:

"At two o'clock to-day an order came for my change of residence and work. Our Lord had already prepared me for it. I offered myself this morning in prayer at the feet of the Blessed Sacrament, and He showed me that it was well. My heart is full of the wish to serve God by the abandonment of self, the crucifixion of all attachments to all earthly things. I hope now to devote my self, body and soul, to the duties of my new position."

At that time he thought his end was at hand. He had been very ill, and had scarcely a breath of life. The least indisposition in his shattered state of health became a source of serious danger.

"I have," he writes, "a presentiment of my speedy decease. What a grace to be able to prepare oneself for it!"

Thus death on all sides seemed to be his portion; yet out of it God brought him to a fuller life.

IV

HIS LIFE WORK REVEALED

"One afternoon in the month of January, 1851" said Blessed Eymard to us only a few days before his death, "I went alone to Notre-Dame de Fourvière. One thought absorbed me so much that I had no other feeling. Our Lord in the Blessed Eucharist seemed to me to have no religious order of men to glorify Him in this mystery of love: I mean no religious body who made *that* their one object, and to which their whole lives should be consecrated. *One is needed.* I promised Mary I would devote myself to carrying out this idea. Still, it was all very vague. And I did not then think of sacrificing my vocation as Marist."... And he added, with an emotion which was indescribable, "Oh, what hours I passed there!"

"Did you then see Our Lady!" one of us exclaimed, "that you were so strongly impressed?"

A half "Yes," extorted by truth, but concealed through humility, came from his lips, but we did not dare question him as to whether this apparition had been sensible and visible or merely an interior manifestation. Whatever it may have been, from that moment the father undertook, with an ardor and tenacity which stopped at no obstacle, the labor of founding an Order expressly for the work of the Blessed Sacrament.

His first idea was to establish an association of men and women attached to the "Third Order" of Mary, which should devote itself to the worship of the Holy Eucharist.

He submitted this project to his venerable Superior in these words: "Let me open my heart to you on a thought which I have struggled against in vain for a long time, but which pursues me without ceasing, and seems to reproach me for resisting the voice of God."

It was a beautiful thought. The great soul of the Very Rev. Jean-Claude Colin understood it at once, and approved of it. But he thought it wiser to defer its execution.

At La Seyne Blessed Eymard was, as it were, haunted by this one idea. Our Lord gave him no rest. They were four years of cruel trial. His strong attraction for the Blessed Eucharist seemed to force itself upon him at every turn. On the other hand, there was his vocation, the arduous duties of his office, the rules of prudence, the orders of his superiors. Who shall say what tortures great souls often go through till they are thoroughly purified, and have learnt to throw themselves unreservedly into the abyss of the Will of God? Our Lord requires blind instruments.

To begin with, however, he had established in the chapel of the house adoration for one day, once a month.

"In my room," he said, "I had a little window looking down on the tabernacle. I passed my nights there. One day," he continued, "there was a whole holiday at the college in honor of St Joseph. I sent all my students out on a long expedition, and then went and said my Mass. During my thanksgiving I was overwhelmed with such joy and sweetness that even now I cannot think of it without tears of thanksgiving." (He was speaking to us in July, 1868.) "It was just after that, while I was still kneeling before the altar, that Our Lord asked me to sacrifice my vocation. I said 'Yes' to everything, and made a vow then and there to devote myself till the hour of my death to found a society of adoration. I promised Our Lord that nothing should stop me, even if I should have only stones to eat and should die in a hospital! Beyond this, I asked of God (though I fear it was presumptuous on my part) to be allowed to labor at this work without any human consolations. The flood of joy which filled my soul when I had made this offering to God gave me a strength and a confidence which sustained me in all my trials." "And they have not been light!" he added, smiling.

In 1853 he had employed a certain eminent personage to consult the Holy Father Pius IX on the whole subject. The Pope replied, "That it was a beautiful thought, and that if it were the will of God to bring it about, he would encourage it as much as lay in his power." But the means to carry out such a project? "Ah, it was a long time under ground 'rotting'!" was the good Father's expression.

"I own," he writes in 1853, "that I should not like to die till I can realize the grand thought which Our Lord has put into my heart regarding the worship of the Blessed Sacrament. It is so sublime an idea that poor human nature shrinks from it, but so beautiful that the thought encourages me to make every sacrifice for it."

On the 10th of May, 1854, he writes again: "Perhaps Our Lord wishes in me only the desire of this great work. But if it be His will I should like to put it into execution." A little later he is more hopeful: "Pray earnestly for this work of the Blessed Sacrament; things are beginning to shape themselves a little; but, above all, we must have men on fire with the love of God. Ask them of Our Lord."

The year 1855 begins, and we find this note in his books: "Let this new year be a Eucharistic one. May a chorus of love and praise arise from this ungrateful and forgetful earth! May I be its first adorer and its first victim!"

Some one objected, "But what will become of the Nazareth of Jesus and Mary?"

He answered, "From Nazareth Jesus passed to the 'upper room' of the Last Supper. And Mary made it her last residence."

Later on in that year he writes again: "The work of the Blessed Sacrament is assuming a definite shape. The rules are drawn up. But what will Our Lord do with me, suffering and worthless as I am? I am no longer good for anything. I am worn out, and need to go and hide myself somewhere. All I hope for is that Our Lord Jesus Christ will let me lie at His feet."

We have alluded to the rules. Blessed Eymard had worked hard at them, and had submitted them to the verdict of a wise and learned friend of his, who replied in these terms: "Your rules as a whole are inspired by a spirit of faith and charity, which is the principal aim and object of the work. You have a right to hope that Our Lord will bestow His blessing on an institution solely devoted to His honor and to increasing the love felt for Him in the Blessed Sacrament."

But this was not enough. From Rome alone come light and truth. Accordingly, in the month of August, he presented a petition to the Holy Father. He gave a sketch of his plan, not concealing the difficulties in its execution; but his words, full of humility and submission, were yet equally full of that strength which arose from the conviction that he was simply following the Will of God.

"Allow me, Most Holy Father," he wrote, "I, the least of your children, to lay at the feet of Your Holiness this my most secret thought. For four years I have resisted this interior feeling, fearing it might arise from human motives or diabolical suggestions; but now I feel I can keep silence no longer. Most Holy Father, at the sight of the love of Jesus Christ in His Adorable Sacrament, of the isolation in which He is left, of the indifference and tepidity of so many Christians, of the growing impiety of men in this age and of the pressing and widely extended needs of the Church, I said to myself: Why should there not be a body of men whose mission should be to pray perpetually at the feet of Jesus Christ in the Most Holy Sacrament of His Love?"

He then went into further details as to the different apostolates which such a society could fulfill, and he ended with these words: "My cause, most Holy Father, is in your hands. I will keep my soul in peace, waiting for that supreme decision, which will be for me a sign of the Divine Will. If Your Holiness does not think such a work should be established, I shall submit myself to your decision with all simplicity, certain that God will have spoken to me by your mouth."

Pius IX replied: "I am convinced that this idea of yours comes from God, and is no delusion. It is a work which the Church needs. Let every means be employed to make the Blessed Sacrament better known."

During this time Blessed Eymard had been sent to the waters of Mont d'Or to be treated for a violent chest attack.

"I arrived here yesterday," he writes. "It is a cold place, where I have not met a single creature I know. I am, therefore, very solitary; but I wished it to be so. With heaven overhead and the Divine Tabernacle close at hand, I have all that I need."

Thus, alone with Jesus, he prepared himself for the greatest sacrifice in his life.

He loved his Order passionately, and he was much beloved by it. To snap asunder ties which had been strengthened by seventeen years of affection and mutual toil is hard. One may leave one's family; that is, after all, but a natural tie. But Jesus Himself is the link of souls in religious life. "The fraternity of Christ," writes St Ambrose, "is closer than the fraternity of blood." This last is founded on human resemblance; the source of the first is identity of souls and hearts.

The bare thought of this separation used to put him into an agony. "My nature is then in the Garden of Olives," he would say; and again, speaking to an intimate friend, he added, "This thought has crucified me for a long while. The filial affection I bear towards the society, towards my superiors, towards my community, their extreme kindness as regards me, and my own weakness, corporal and spiritual, all urge me to be quiet. On the other hand, I feel I cannot do otherwise than correspond with the grace of God if He deigns to call me to labor and die for this great work. And I am attracted to it so strongly that, at times, I feel as if I could not draw back." And again:

"God exacts of me the sacrifice of my dear Society, because when I became a religious the first time I had only to make the sacrifice of my father and my sister. I shall always remain the child of the Society in gratitude and devotion. Who can forget so good and tender a mother?" In 1856 these terrible mental struggles were to come to an end. It was more than his mind and heart could bear for a longer period: often he would exclaim, "I am the victim of a delusion; the serpent deceived me. Lord, send him whom Thou hast chosen.... I am not worthy of this charge.... I will abandon myself entirely into God's hands, act as if I had no plan, and in all my prayers and hopes leave *myself* out of the question."

This was the moment of God's grace. He molded the will of his Superior; and Blessed Eymard was sent to Paris, there to make a retreat, under the direction of a certain eminent ecclesiastic, so as to arrive at a final decision. He did not even know the name of the community to which he was sent; for he writes on the 1st of May: "I know neither the name nor the work of these good Fathers to whom I have been sent; it seems to be a new community of the Trappist kind. But the Tabernacle is there—that supplies all my wants." He opened his whole heart on the object he had in view in making this retreat:

"I am come to make up my mind once and forever on a question which for many years has caused me intense suffering, trial and preoccupation. As it is not simply an attraction which I feel, but a question of conscience, or one which I believe to be such, I want to have my mind enlightened, and, therefore, to consult a perfect stranger. I shall submit to his decision, whatever it may be. I shall pray earnestly before choosing him, and then remain in perfect peace. I want to rid myself of all thoughts of self, of all my own thoughts, wishes, and plans, and all that might favor a decision in accordance with natural inclinations. If God, in His infinite goodness and wisdom, says to me, 'Go on—go up to Calvary,' with His grace, and with His love, I will complete the sacrifice. If, on the contrary, on account of unworthiness, Our Lord tells me to return to Lyons, I shall go back instantly, without any other regret than not to have been found worthy to serve more directly Jesus, that great King of Love."

The trial lasted till the 13th of May. It seemed the grave of his hopes. But Our Lord was about to bring about their resurrection.

He writes in a note:

"After twelve days of prayer, of tears, of entire abandonment of myself into the hands of God, the trial is at an end.

"Three bishops were to judge the question. The Bishop of Tripoli and the Bishop of Carcassone (Monsignor François-Alexandre de la Bouillerie) were to examine it from a religious and personal point of view; to the Archbishop of Paris was to be reserved the final decision, and to pronounce his opinion after consultation with the other two."

Blessed Eymard, with the utmost simplicity, calmness, and exact truthfulness, set before them his reasons, his difficulties, and the arguments for and against the proposal. Everything seemed to oppose itself to his views; he felt as if the Bishops were against him, and he had made the sacrifice in his own heart of the whole thing, when, to his intense surprise, the following judgment was delivered:

"The will of God, as regards Father Eymard, has been too clearly manifested to leave any doubt as to the foundation of this Eucharistic work. Our Lord has Himself solved the difficulty. You must henceforth consecrate yourself without hesitation to this work alone."

The three venerable prelates were unanimous in their opinion; and Monsignor Marie-Dominique Sibour blessed Pierre-Julien Eymard and his companion with special tenderness.

"You are my very own children from this hour!" he exclaimed. "May God abundantly bless you and your new work!"

Blessed Eymard and his companion left the Archbishop's house overwhelmed with surprise and gratitude. They went to Saint-Sulpice to pour out their hearts in thanksgiving at the foot of the Tabernacle, and to offer themselves body and soul henceforth to the service of Jesus in the Sacred Host by the hands of Mary, the Queen of the Cenacle.

V

FOUNDATION OF THE CONGREGATION OF THE BLESSED SACRAMENT

"Duc in altum!" It was Our Lord Himself who, by the mouth of authority, had pronounced those words. Blessed Eymard went on, and, strengthened by a might not his own, no future obstacle could retard his course.

As for sacrifices, had he not already felt their sting?

"If I were a saint," he writes, "I should ask our good God to crucify us still more—to annihilate us, in fact, so that His glory alone should be made manifest, and His grace only exalted."

To *annihilate* himself—this is the aim henceforth of all his efforts; it is the keynote of his work.

To understand his life and his conduct we must hold that thread—it leads everywhere. Out of nothing he will establish the omnipotent reign of Jesus Christ; for "nothingness is everything" was one of his favorite sayings.

Providence took care of his children—he had only two at first. Peter and John; but the "supper-room" was ready.

The Archbishop, in his kind anxiety for the immediate establishment of the work, had given them an enclosure formerly occupied by some religious of the Sacred Heart, whose work had failed; so that "the place of trial became the scene of his triumph."

The first thing was to enlarge the sanctuary. This work absorbed the rest of the year. In the meantime a parlor was turned into a chapel; a few boards made the altar, covered with calico; and Jesus did not disdain the little wooden tabernacle, poorer than the stable at Bethlehem. He deigned to take up His abode there on June 1, 1856. On that day, at the Church of St Thomas Aquinas, Monsignor Sibour announced to the members of the Nocturnal Adoration the work which had just been begun for the Blessed Sacrament, which news was received with intense joy by the whole assembly.

The illustrious preacher of the Conferences at Notre Dame, Father Felix, developed, with his usual eloquence and authority, the principles of the new foundation in the following words:

"To save society we must revive the spirit of sacrifice; and it is only by drawing from its source, the Blessed Eucharist, that we can hope to obtain this result. The news given to us, therefore, by the Archbishop, of the foundation of a society of men specially and entirely devoted to the adoration of Jesus in His Sacrament of Love, ought to fill every Christian heart with joy and hope."

In the beginning of January, 1857, Blessed Eymard was able to expose the Blessed Sacrament and to fulfill the principal duties of his new vocation. On the day of the Epiphany, which witnessed the adoration of the Magi at the feet of the Great Master, Our Lord mounted His Eucharistic throne. Members of almost all the religious orders were represented on this pious occasion, and seemed to greet thus with sympathy and affection the birth of their new sister. The Confraternity of the Nocturnal Adoration were among the first to hasten to the little sanctuary, and in great numbers. Blessed Eymard preached, and began with these words:

"One day St John the Baptist received a deputation from the chief priests of the Jews, who asked him, *Tu qui es?* It seems to me, brethren, that your presence here today seems to ask us the same question: 'Who are you?' 'What is this new work?'

"To the first question I answer, Nothing! and may we be ever as nonentities in the hands of God! We have nothing which contributes to the glory, the success, or the power of a work. If we had been cradled in human greatness, or were under such protection as insures victory, I should fear that God was not with us.

"We have one supreme protection—we began with the special blessing of the Church and its Head.

"But 'what is this new work?'

"It is the Society of the Most Holy Sacrament. 'Religious of the Blessed Sacrament'—this is the name we have taken. Our object is to glorify the Blessed Eucharist; the means, the perpetual exposition of the Adorable Sacrament. We do not refuse all external apostolate; but we limit it to those ministrations which bear more immediately on our one noble end."

From that day the Blessed Sacrament was exposed three times a week. It could not be oftener, because vocations were rare; many tried, but few remained; and Blessed Eymard accepted this trial with his usual simple faith. "It is not for us to give vocations," he would say. "Now that the seed is sown, we have only to let it rot in the earth till it takes root, and springs into fresh life when God's hour is come."

A new sort of trial awaited the work very few months after its commencement. They had to leave their little Bethlehem. For more than a year they hunted in vain through every corner of Paris. No suitable place could be found. Often they fancied they had obtained what they wanted. Vain hope! One day an admirable chapel for the exposition was offered them, but without any house for priests alongside. "What a consolation!" exclaimed Blessed Eymard. "We shall begin by lodging Our Dear Lord—the King—before His servants; that is just and right! He is sure to find us a lodging later, He is so good!" But this scheme again fell through. "Lord Jesus, help us!" they cried. "All that remains to us is to lift up our suppliant hands to Thee." He had other subjects of anxiety, which amounted at times to perfect agony of mind. We may judge of his feelings from the ejaculatory prayers which at this time he wrote down in his journal, and which show the severity of the trial through which he was passing:

"Bone Jesu, salva nos, perimus! Hoc solum habemus residui ut oculos nostros dirigamus ad Te!"

"O bone Magister, ubi, quando, quomodo Tu volueris!"

"Loquere, Domine, et ne derelinquas nos."

"Domine, vim patior, responde pro me."

"Domine Jesu, tristis est anima mea usque ad desolationem et fletum."

"Da mihi victoriam, O Rex crucifixus amore; vincam caritate."

"Salva nos, Domine Jesu! Vince, regna, impera solus," etc.

All these trials, however, only strengthened him. He was ready to drink to the last drop the chalice of suffering, provided that the Will of God should triumph. *"Fiat voluntas Tua"* was ever on his lips and in his heart. And Jesus was with him; and with Jesus, hell itself would be paradise. *"Mane nobiscum, Domine, et sufficit nobis; et humiliatio et solitudo erunt paradisus voluptatis."*

At last his faith and love conquered, and Our Lord seemed, as it were, to point out where His Tabernacle should be set up. It was a chapel of the Faubourg Saint-Jacques. During the concluding negotiations, however, the devil employed every device to stop it, and several times he seemed to be on the point of succeeding. Blessed Eymard appealed to Our Lord to defend His own glory. "All seems again lost," he wrote. "Shall the devil triumph through our mistakes and inexperience? Thy glory, O Lord, is at stake. Exalt Thyself in our nothingness!"

On Easter Sunday, 1858, the Great King appeared once more enthroned above His tabernacle. He remained there nine years, and poured out His graces in such profusion that the little sanctuary obtained the name of the "Chapel of Miracles."

(When a future revolution had driven Our Lord away, Blessed Eymard came back one day to pray in this blessed spot. At the sight of the broken windows and the riven walls, he fell on his knees and exclaimed with tears, "Let us join with the angels, who weep over the desolate ruins of this once holy sanctuary.")

To the blessing of having at last a resting-place Our Lord soon added another. In the month of December, Blessed Eymard laid at the feet of the Holy Father the first-fruits of the precious encouragement which had fallen from his lips three years before, presenting at the same time the flattering letters he had received from the greater part of the venerable bishops of France.

Pius IX blessed afresh the work and its author, granted it precious Indulgences, and signed the laudatory Brief with his own hand:

"Beloved son, it has been supremely agreeable to us to hear of the zeal with which, for the last three years, you have labored to promote the worship and increase the adoration of the Adorable Sacrament, especially in France. The letters from the bishops are striking witnesses of this fact, and of the success of your new work. May Our Lord, in His mercy, bless and fructify the labors undertaken for this end, which have elicited universal praise! And may the Apostolical Benediction which you have solicited from us, and which we gladly give to our beloved son in the effusion of our paternal love, be a pledge of your success and of the increase of so great a good!"

The words of Pius IX were fertile; the Society of the Blessed Sacrament was asked for and received, the following year, with the most touching kindness, by Monsignor Eugène de Mazenod of holy memory, Bishop of Marseille; and the faithful in that Catholic city surrounded the new Eucharistic foundation with a devotion and a pious enthusiasm which from that hour to this have never slackened, but gone on increasing day by day.

In 1862 Blessed Eymard had obtained enough subjects to be able to open a regular novitiate. This is the time to give a short account of his spirit, his rules, and his doctrine; a few extracts will suffice.

VI

LIFE OF THE FATHERS OF THE BLESSED SACRAMENT

In establishing the Society of the Most Holy Sacrament, Blessed Eymard wished, as it were, to create a Community whose aim should be a logical consequence of the Real Presence of Our Lord in the Eucharist.

Our Lord, though He has deigned thus to annihilate Himself, is still King of heaven and earth. He has a right to a solemn and continual service, which should correspond, as far as this miserable earth can do, to the glorious adoration of the angels and saints in heaven, and of which He makes the sacrifice when He condescends to dwell among men.

But ordinary Christians cannot give up their duties and their work without disturbing the social order. So Blessed Eymard resolved to select and unite certain men of good-will, who should compose *a court on earth* for our hidden yet celestial King. He thus explains his plans: "Our Lord will be taken from His Tabernacle. He will be exposed. He will reign. He will be the Master; and He will have servants, whose sole occupation will be the care of His Divine Person, leaving all other work for the service of His Throne and for the needs of His Royal Presence. These religious will give Him *personal* service and not indirectly by their works. Others, fired by a noble passion for martyrdom, fly beyond the seas, and carry light and life to nations sitting in the shadow of death; or consume their lives in training children to be faithful and earnest Christians; or fight, by their preaching and their writings, against the false doctrines and the fatal prejudices of the century. But the religious who belongs to the Court of the King honors only His Presence. He is His Chamberlain, one of His bodyguard. So whilst the valiant soldiers of the Cross are fighting the battles of God and His Church, he has nothing else to do but this: to take care that the Master is never left alone.

"Let all our religious understand clearly," writes Blessed Eymard, "that they have been chosen, and have made their profession, solely to devote themselves to the service of the Divine Person of Jesus Christ our King and our God, who is visibly, really, and substantially present in the Sacrament of His Love. Therefore, like good and faithful servants of so great a King, they must consecrate to His greater glory their qualities, their virtues, their studies, their work, without anything *personal*."

This service embraces different kinds of duties. A king needs a palace, heralds, courtiers. So both in the priesthood and the laity a vast field is opened out for the service of their King, and varied occupations to suit the aptitudes of each.

All are to meet and live in common, without any privileges. It is the model of family life, animated solely by the spirit of Divine Love, which binds them together as members of one body devoted to the personal service of one Master.

"Our Lord," continues Blessed Eymard "has many kinds of servants. Some labor for His glory abroad, others He wishes to be exclusively devoted to His adorable Person. He has called us to follow Him, but it must be to attend upon Him alone. This absolute service has been the condition of your admission. The law of your life, the perfection of your holiness, *is to serve*. You are not come here to sanctify yourselves in solitude, or to be apostles, or to save souls by leading them to God through a wise and prudent direction. You are come solely to wait upon our Lord. As He has attached His apostles to their missions, so He has bound you to His Person. Your duty is ever to surround the Blessed Eucharist. If *It* cease to be, we should no longer have any reason ourselves for existing.... So as to be exclusively attached to the royal service of our King, and always ready to take their turn of adoration, our religious must keep themselves independent and free from all other employment, and all servitude to individuals. They will not be employed in long services or in extraneous functions, such as preaching or the direction of souls, which would diminish their fervor in their adoration."

"When you came to knock at the door of this holy refuge," said Blessed Eymard one day to his young novices, "did any one ask you what talent you had? or what degree of ability? or if you had done such or such good works? 'No.' You were asked only, 'Who sent you?' 'Jesus Christ.' 'To whom do you wish to come?' 'To Jesus Christ.' 'Have you any conditions to make?' 'None.' 'Then come, and come in quickly.' You were invited to join in the adoration. 'Will you put yourself on this *prie-dieu* and burn there, like the wax-taper on the altar? Will you be the servant of our Lord?' 'Yes.' 'Then come.' You were further told to go directly to Our Lord for advice and direction. He alone is the Master. Let Him alone be your Superior. We are content to be His vicars, His John the Baptists sent to tell you, *'He is there';* and then retire when we have introduced you. Serve Him, then, devotedly, and be at peace as to the rest. As long as He is pleased with you *and* will keep you in His service no one else will have anything to say to you.... Three times a day the religious are on duty before Our Lord. They follow in turn all the hours of the clock, so as to participate in the fresh joy of the morning, the soft melancholy of evening, and the religious, gravity of night."

"Look upon the hour which has fallen to your portion," he writes again, "as an hour of paradise. Go to it as to the banquet of God. Say to yourself often during the day, 'In four, three, or two hours I shall be admitted to an audience of Our Lord. He has invited me. He waits for me.' Should the hour, when it arrives, be painful to your poor human nature, rejoice in it all the more. This will be a privileged hour and count for two. If from some infirmity, sickness, or other cause, it is impossible for you to make your hour's adoration, let your heart feel sadness for a while; but then unite yourself in spirit with him who has taken your place." Those who saw him, the instant the bell sounded, hurrying to his hour of watching, and at the kneeling-stool remaining immovable, scarcely touching the rail, his eyes fixed with ardent, yet respectful, love on the Divine Host, understood that, while teaching his novices, he was unconsciously describing his own method of adoration.

"In the very presence of Our Lord," he would say, "will you be generous in your love? Speak to Him of Himself. Speak to Him of His Divine Father, of the works He undertook for His glory, and you will rejoice His Heart. Speak to Him of His Love for men, and you will fill Him with joy. Speak to Jesus of His Mother, and you will gratify His affection as a Son. Speak to Him of His Saints, and you will then exalt His graces in them. Having thus spoken to Jesus of Himself, He will then speak to you. Your heart will expand under the rays of this Sun of goodness as the flower, wet with dew, opens on a summer morning. You will listen to Him, then, in silence and peace, or rather in the sweetest action of love. *You will live in Him.* What hinders the growth of this grace in us is, that scarcely are we at the feet of our Divine Master than we spread out before Him our wants, our sins, our miseries, and thus weary both heart and mind. Let your first movement, then, be, 'O my good Jesus, how happy I am to come and see Thee and to be allowed to spend this next hour with Thee! How kind of Thee to have called me! How good Thou art to love such a poor creature as I am! I will try to make Thee some return of love!'

"Then love will have opened to you the Heart of Our Lord. Enter, love, and adore.

"But you ask, 'What subject can I find for an adoration which recurs so frequently?'

"*Assueta vilescunt.* Alas, routine deadens even our love of God!

"But will you have the secret of Eucharistic prayer? Look through the divine prism of this mystery at all the truths, all the virtues, of our holy religion.

"*The Blessed Eucharist is Jesus Christ, past, present, and future.*

"It is the royal mystery of faith, wherein all Catholic truths flow, as the streams empty themselves into the great ocean.

"What more simple than to compare the birth of Jesus in the stable with His sacramental birth on our altars and in our hearts?

"Who does not understand that the hidden life at Nazareth is continued in the Divine Host of the tabernacle?

"Or that the passion of the Man-God on Calvary is renewed in the Holy Sacrifice, at each moment of its existence? Is not Our Lord gentle and humble in the Blessed Sacrament, as He was during His mortal life? Is He not always there as the good pastor, the Divine consoler, the friend of our hearts? Happy the soul who knows where to find Jesus in the Blessed Eucharist, and in the Eucharist all other things!

"There indeed Our Lord is both priest and king. 'One personally, He is morally universal,' writes Jean-Jacques Olier; 'that is, He unites in Himself the homages and desires of all His members, and our prayers have no merit save in union with the prayer of Jesus Christ.'

"The supreme prayer of Our Lord is the Holy Sacrifice of the Mass, wherein He presents to the Eternal Father an infinite homage of *adoration,* a host of *thanksgiving,* a victim of *propitiation,* and a *prayer,* which obtains all it asks.

"Such are the four ends of the Sacrifice of the Altar: to *adore, give thanks, ask for pardon, and pray.*"

The soul which fully enters into these four objects is clothed, as it were, with the very prayer of Jesus Christ, and has attained to the perfection of Eucharistic devotion. To explain this method of adoration was Father Eymard's great object. But he would not constrain any one to practice it. "The best method of prayer," he writes in his Rules, "is that which the Holy Spirit Himself inspires in a pure and humble soul."

"But, in truth, there is no mystery on which we can meditate at the feet of Our Lord which does not give matter for *adoration, thanksgiving, reparation* and *prayer*. There is no virtue which we cannot *adore* in Our Lord, and for which we may not *thank* Him for being the model; and then, turning to ourselves, how can we be otherwise than *humbled* at resembling our Master so little? or fail to utter the prayer, 'O Jesus, forgive! and grant us to grow in Thy grace and in the imitation of Thy virtues'?"

This is the summary of Blessed Eymard's method of adoration, the four ends of the Sacrifice. "One hour thus spent seems but an instant!" he exclaimed. "Astonished at having so soon to leave one's *prie-dieu*, one thinks only of the happy moment which will bring one back to it."

To these hours of adoration the religious of the Blessed Sacrament add the public recital of the Divine Office; a solemn act of adoration likewise, in which the whole court surrounds the King, and sings His praises in the words of the Holy Spirit. Besides this direct homage of praise to his Master, he is likewise a royal servant; whether priest, or layman, he takes care of the house of the King and everything pertaining to it, and does his best to extend the kingdom of Jesus Christ in the souls of men.

At each hour of the day a bell warns him to salute, on his knees, wherever he may be, the Most Holy and Divine Sacrament, a watchword which recalls to his mind the near presence of his King. To sustain his fervor, he adds an affectionate salutation to the Queen of the supper-room, the Blessed Virgin Mary. The following are the invocations, enriched with Indulgences for all the faithful:

"Blessed and praised every moment be the most Holy and Most Divine Sacrament."

"And blessed be the Holy and Immaculate Conception of the Blessed Virgin Mary."

The spirit of this service—the livery, if we may so speak, worn by these servants with the arms of their Master—is forgetfulness of self, personal abnegation; in a word, *self-annihilation.*

"The characteristic virtue of a priest of the Blessed Sacrament and that which proves the reality and depth of his vocation, is one which is supremely Eucharistic, and of which Our Lord gives us a never-ceasing model. He annihilates Himself, taking the form, not of a slave, but of a bit of common bread."

"Our Lord hides His Divine and human glory in the Most Holy Sacrament.

"Our Lord unites with it His Divine and human power.

"Our Lord renounces in it all possessions in heaven and in earth.

"Our Lord immolates His will.

"Our Lord veils even His virtues, His goodness, His love, His gentleness and sweetness.

"Vere Deus absconditus—Our God is truly a hidden God.

"Such is the model of the virtue of the religious adorer.

"This virtue sanctifies his whole soul, all his senses, his whole life. It is in union with the sacramental state of Our Blessed Lord. Through it he gives himself up to Jesus Christ, to dispose as He wills of his life and his person. He becomes a member of His body; he gives proof of his love; he gives himself for love.

"This is the whole of the holiness and the glory Our Lord asks of us or by us. To annihilate ourselves, so that He may be exalted; to efface ourselves, so that He alone may appear; to become as the sacramental species, which certainly has no pride and pretends to no glory, as it has no life of its own.

"In other words, it is to live in an absolute dependence on Our Lord, and to leave to Him the initiative in all things.

"The practical rule of our conduct is this: 'What does Our Lord

Jesus Christ want of us at this moment?'

"In this thought, in this desire, in this action, is there anything for His service, for His glory? What would Our Lord do on such or such an occasion?

"During the course of His mortal life Our Lord refused to do anything of Himself: 'I do nothing of Myself' (John viii. 28). His doctrine is not His own, but that of His Father. Men wish to exalt Him; He refuses all honor. He will not even allow Himself to be called 'good'; 'None is good but God alone' (Luke xviii. 19). Our Lord will not suffer any one for an instant to exalt Him as man, or to make Him a *human* personality, which He willed should be entirely absorbed in the personality of the Word.

"Well, these essential words in our constitutions, *Absque sui proprio,* put us in the way of participating, as much as poor imperfect creatures can do, in the sacrifice of the personality of Jesus Christ.

"This thought is as old as the Christian world: we certainly have not invented it. It is the *Vivo, jam non ego,* of St Paul. The saints realized it in their daily life; we only want to make it the distinguishing virtue of a religious body.

"To serve, not only by our works, but by ourselves, costs a good deal; and yet if we would arrive at being 'all for Jesus,' we must be all through Him and by Him. Thus we give the tree and its fruits. It is thus we learn to accept all sacrifices, natural and spiritual. Ah, remember that you have left all, and have given yourselves to the service of Our Lord without reserve or condition. Do not rob your Master, then, either for your mind or for your body. Give Him your intelligence. Let all your studies tend to Him. You ought to have no science but that of the Blessed Sacrament. Do all your thoughts tend towards the Eucharist?

"And your heart should be all for Jesus in the Blessed Eucharist. Do you care for anything outside this service or anything which is opposed to it? Remember you have no more claim on human love;

and if a soul attaches itself to yours, even with a good motive and to draw nearer to Jesus, yet beware. Remember you have renounced your personality. Your body belongs to your Master as much as your soul. Whenever you seek consolation outside Jesus Christ, you take back your offering. 'It is enough for the disciple that he be as his Master, and the servant as his Lord' (Matt. x. 25).

"You have not been admitted into this society," he would say to his novices, "to become good and virtuous men, nor even to increase the amount of your merits, or to obtain greater glory in heaven; for then you would yourselves be the object of your service. You are come solely to immolate yourselves, body and soul, to the service of your Eucharistic King, so as to procure for Him the greatest glory possible by the homage of a love which goes to the extent of heroism in its personal sacrifice as the simple and natural expression of its duty.

"Your great merit, then, will be perpetually to give your whole selves, body, soul, and spirit and to feel that when you have done even heroic acts of virtue, you have only done that which it was your duty to do — that is, you have conducted yourselves as is meet and fitting in the presence of your great King.

"All praise, all merit, must return to Jesus, your Master. A soldier wins the battle and dies — who thinks of him? The king alone has the glory and the triumph.

"Do not be afraid. We shall be enough rewarded by and by. If we forget ourselves for Our Lord, He will not forget us. In the meantime let our sole preoccupation be to serve Him, and to give ourselves entirely to Him. After all, one does this continually in daily life, and without giving it a thought. Does a mother think anything of her incessant devotion to her child? Does she expect him to pay a price for it? And the same with a loving husband or wife; even with a friend to a friend.

"Well, do not let us have less self-devotion towards Our Lord. May He exclaim when He sees us at His feet. 'Ah, they love Me for Myself alone!'"

VII

HIS EUCHARISTIC PREACHING

We hope we have not wearied our readers with these quotations; but in order to understand Blessed Eymard's work we must penetrate its spirit. He would often say: "We must both serve and fight. Our first object is to be a bodyguard to honor our King on His throne. But He is also exposed; and we must strive and bring innumerable other adorers to His feet. The Blessed Eucharist is the burning flame He is come to enkindle in the earth. It is not a question of defending a certain article of faith, but the God of Truth, who is everywhere attacked. It is not the moment to make profession of such or such a virtue; we must show men how Our Lord is abandoned in the Sacrament of His love. We must preach the Divine Eucharist in season and out of season, here, there, and everywhere. In all our intercourse with other men, in all our exterior acts, let Our Lord have His part: *Dum omni modo Christus annuntietur* (Phil. i. 18).

"Each flower has its form, its color, its perfume. Shall we ever be weary of enjoying them? In the same way in heaven there is always the same hymn of glory and praise which rejoices the city of God. So must the adorer preach forever Jesus in the Blessed Eucharist, that mystery of faith, of sweetness, and of beauty."... "Learn to understand the full meaning of the Blessed Sacrament," he often repeated to his priests. "It is a mine in which you may dig forever. Let your hours of adoration bring forth fruit. If any one understands this mystery better than we do, let us yield our *prie-dieu* to him. We are not worthy of our place there."

Blessed Eymard never preached without passing a long time before the tabernacle. He used to write a few notes, and especially studied the Gospel of St John, which he had continually in his heart and on his lips. He called this preliminary work "kneading the flour," which, when exposed after to the Eucharistic fire, became "solid bread," fit to give to his hearers. Often, however, inspired by a sudden light, he would leave the subject he had prepared for another. "I am persuaded," wrote an eminent preacher, after hearing one of his sermons, "that this father spoke to-day under the direct inspiration of the Holy Spirit." He used to tell his priests that their sermons should be "adorations made out loud," and this was eminently the case with his own. The odd thing was that he never could remember, when he left the pulpit, what he had said. One day he was overwhelmed with enthusiastic congratulations on a sermon he had preached before a very distinguished audience. He looked annoyed and confused, and said to an intimate friend, "That he really did not know what they meant; for he had no part whatever in the instruction he had given. He preached only the words which were put into his mouth at the moment." Once he saw a summary of one of his sermons which he had given the day before. "Who said all these fine things?" he asked. "Why, it was your yesterday's lecture!" "I never should have guessed it," he simply replied, and quickly turned the subject. A celebrated ecclesiastic once said to him, "Why do you not give a more careful form to your sermons, of which the groundwork is so rich and admirable?" But this was contrary to his fixed resolve. He had from the first begged Our Lord "that no words of his should fix public attention on himself"; and his ideal ambition was that people should say, after hearing him, "What good and pure water comes through that old worm-eaten wooden pipe!"

"Beware of pretension of any sort," he would say to his young preachers. "Be as simple as possible. Recollect Our Lord will not suffer you to raise up a throne for yourselves alongside of His own."

He preached everywhere on the same subject. At Rouen, Nantes, Rennes, during retreats—it was always on the glories of the Blessed Eucharist and the profit which Christians should derive from Holy Communion. To the Benedictines of Pierre-qui-Vire, who have revived a penitential system which seems impossible to our self-indulgent age, the father gave Our Lord as the model of their austere and crucified lives. "You have embraced a state of living death," he said, "It is the state of Jesus in the Eucharist."

Giving a retreat to some young men who had just been ordained, he developed during those eight days these fundamental thoughts: "A priest should be a saint. It is only the God of the Eucharist who makes saints. What does holiness mean but the life of Our Lord substituted for our corrupt nature? Customs are sucked in with our mother's milk. Holy Communion will inoculate in us the mind, the virtues, the habits of Jesus Christ. It was only after the Last Supper that Jesus said to His Apostles, 'Whatsoever I have heard of My Father I have made known unto you' (John xv. 15). It was only then that the Apostles began to comprehend a little Our Lord's meaning."

The priest is a man of devotion and sacrifice. But is not the Eucharist the supreme sacrifice? devotion carried to its highest pitch?

"Let a priest put himself under this press of love, and he will exclaim, with St Paul, 'The love of Christ urges us.' From the altar of self-devotion there is but one step, as from the love-feasts in the catacombs to the torments of the circus."

In 1862 he was invited to preach the novena for the Feast of the Sacred Heart at Saint-Sulpice, at Paris. "What is Jesus Christ?" he exclaimed on this occasion. "It is the incarnation of the love of God for man, personified in a human nature and perpetuated in the Blessed Eucharist." Then he showed what was the Heart of Jesus: His ardent desire to give Himself to us in the Sacrament of His love; the institution of the Last Supper in the extreme effusion of that love; and then its perpetuation in the Blessed Sacrament out of love for man, in spite of his indifference, his ingratitude, and his sacrileges.

We cannot analyze all these sermons; and will conclude with this word, taken from his personal notes, and which gives a summary of his whole apostleship:

"Jesus Christ is there! Then let us give ourselves wholly to Him."

VIII

EUCHARISTIC APOSTOLATE

"All for Jesus in the Blessed Eucharist!" To arrive at this, Blessed Eymard resolved to place every class of society under the direct influence of this sun of love. Three distinct works were the result.

Through the work of the *First Communion of Poor Adults,* as it was called, he was able to bring back to the feet of Our Lord many hundreds of perishing souls.

Through the *Aggregation to the Most Holy Sacrament,* he gave to the faithful, as it were, a crown and a center to their labors by uniting them with the adorers of the Divine Eucharist.

As to the first-mentioned work, we will give its object in his own words:

"The object of this work, which Monsignor Sibour accepted so joyfully for his diocese, is to hunt up, instruct, and prepare for their first Communion all adults who have passed the age of the ordinary parochial catechisms or instructions; or who, by the long hours in their workshops, have been unable to attend them.

"The number of young men who have not made their first Communion is very great—at Paris they may be reckoned by hundreds. Many amongst them have not even been baptized. A youth who has thus never received any primary Christian teaching is generally lost. He follows the leadings of his passions. A bad son first, he becomes, later on, a bad husband, a bad father, and almost invariably a dangerous citizen. To. earn his daily bread is the sole law of his life. He knows neither God his Father, nor Jesus Christ his Saviour, nor the Holy Ghost his Sanctifier. He is, in reality, a savage, with all the vices of civilization.... The best recruiting sergeants in this work I have found to be children. Grateful for the care and affection which have been shown to them, they will almost invariably, after the Sunday which has witnessed their own great joy, bring an older friend or companion to take their place.

"How often have they come back with their father or their mother, their elder brothers or sisters, each begging in turn for instruction and to receive Holy Communion! But, even if they do not go so far, one obtains, through the children, easy access to the parents. They are proud to assist at the feast of their sons; and there is not one of them, later on, who falls sick, who does not send one of these very children to fetch the priest. How many marriages, again, have been the fruit of the first Communions of the children! They are really the apostles of their poor families."

It was touching to see him in the evening, after Divine Office, sitting in the midst of those ragged, weary young workmen, saying a loving word to each; encouraging and cheering them with all his might; and then distributing to them the bread of Christian truth. They knew neither God nor themselves.

He had the gift of fixing their attention and overcoming all indifference by a few simple, original, incisive words. Before the day of their first Communion arrived he had made them understand the great mysteries of the faith, the duties of a child of God, the obligations of a good son, and the duties of an honest man towards his neighbor; and very often the final examination went so far beyond what one could have expected from minds worn out with precocious toil, without a day's rest from work, either for body or soul, since they were children.

The great day of the first Communion having arrived, Blessed

Eymard would go himself to their employers, and ask for a day's holiday for them as a special favor to himself. Sometimes he would obtain two. He then gave a kind of little retreat. Three times a day Father Eymard would speak to them, explaining the full meaning of confession, and making them long more than ever for their Sacramental Lord. "What I want to see in you," he would say, "is a more intimate knowledge of Jesus Christ. Without that, your first Communion will be useless. You have been taught in your catechism who He is. You have Him in your heads. Now you must put Him in your hearts. My poor dear children, you have a hard fight before you in this life. You know it already by experience; and you know how you are surrounded with enemies. But you do not know that you have a Friend *always* at hand? *always* ready to help you? He is here. He is Jesus Christ. He is ever near you. But when you are in church you are in His house. Look at Him here. He is out of His tabernacle, listening to us who are speaking of Him, waiting to hear what you have to say to Him. You see the candles burning? Well, when you pass by a window at night and see a light, you say, 'There is somebody at home in that room.' The light is the sign of a living presence. Well, that is the case here: God is here. When there are no candles burning there is a little lamp. When you come into a church, then; look for that lamp. Our dear Lord and Master Jesus Christ is there! Salute Him by going on your knees; and if you see Him being carried in the streets by His priest, again kneel down. Would you be ashamed of your Saviour? of your King?

"You know who He is now; but that is not enough. You must love Him; for He loves you, even more tenderly than your mother ever did. Do you not believe in this great love of Our Lord for you?... When he actually died for you?... But you reply, 'What will He give me if I love Him?' 'You don't mean that you only recognize affection by big pennies?' 'No. But I have nothing which can possibly attract our Lord to love me!' That is quite true, my poor children; and the world seeks for nothing but its own interests, and doesn't care a farthing for you. Provided you do your day's work, that's all it cares for. But our good God—oh, that is very different! He loves you with an infinite love, because you represent to Him His dear Son Jesus Christ, a poor and humble workman like you. He made Himself not only a man, but a carpenter's son, toiling for His daily bread, hungering, thirsting, wearying Himself—*for you!* It is He who gives you all—health, strength, life itself. He has given you your mother—you love her, do you not? Well, you will love still more Our Lord, who gave and preserves her to you." So he would go on, familiarly, tenderly, varying his illustrations to suit his hearers.

And then came the great day. They are all there, crowding round the altar. Blessed Eymard has made a collection among certain charitable souls to dress them properly on that occasion. Each has a wax taper in his hand, and a medal of our Blessed Lady on his breast. Many of the parents come, too, proud and happy at the honor shown to their sons. They feel they are loved and cared for; and that touches even the most hardened amongst them.

Blessed Eymard himself reads some short and simple prayers to them on the Sacrifice which is about to be offered; and then says a few last words of exhortation:

"Rejoice, my dearly loved children. This is the most beautiful day of your lives—it is the day of God. You are the princes at this feast. We have given up even the sanctuary to you. What are you going to give to Our Lord? Not much, certainly. It is He who will give you all. He will give you Himself, my poor children—*Himself!* You cannot comprehend this mystery. But who can comprehend God? Do you understand how the bread you eat, made of grains and wheat, ground and baked, gives you blood and flesh? No. Yet it is so; for God has given that power to human food. Can He not, then, impart a like power to the Body of Jesus Christ? Ah, yes; you believe it. I know you do. When Our Lord is in you, you will tell Him all the good things you know; you will thank Him, above all, for coming to you. It is not difficult to receive Him; He will help you and bear you. All He asks is that we should be with Him.

After the Communion he always had a comfortable breakfast prepared for them. All the day was spent joyously; and generally a large number of them received the additional Sacrament of Confirmation, while all renewed their baptismal vows, and were consecrated to Our Lady.

In speaking of this work, Blessed Eymard said:

"It is true that some do not persevere; but many come back. Every year they are invited to return and make their Easter duty. They almost invariably accept this invitation. They feel they are cared for and loved. And there is a special pleasure in coming back to the church or chapel where they have made their first Communion. In every case that day has been a marked one, a point in their lives. Later on they will be married in church; and when the hour of sickness and trial comes, there will be a recollection which will touch their hearts, and enable us to have access to them; for that solemn moment is never altogether forgotten."

In fact, this was his favorite work. "I would not give it up for all the world!" he exclaimed one day, when a friend was remonstrating with him on the fatigue it gave him. Even if he could not take all the catechizing on himself, he insisted on hearing their confessions, as well as presiding at their little retreat and their first Communions.

Besides that, he had always some old men to teach, which he did privately; or some ill-assorted couple to instruct and guide. He used to do this at night, after wearisome days, with a devotion and tenderness which showed itself in extreme delicacy towards these poor people. Then he would baptize them or marry them, or give them Holy Communion; but in secret, so as not to wound their susceptibilities or expose them to ill-natured tongues.

In 1868, he came back one February afternoon in the pouring rain, tired to death, and with a violent attack of inflammation of the chest. He had gone a long way out of Paris to bless a marriage of two of these his children, who had previously been living in sin. "You ought not to have gone out so far in such weather, ill as you are," exclaimed his priests on his return. "That is true," he replied gently. "But those poor people; they were so happy, and are so good now!"

IX

THE PRIESTS' EUCHARISTIC LEAGUE

"Oh! Priests, priests!" Blessed Eymard exclaimed one day, "I would leave all for priests!" Full of respect for the priesthood, and always ready to serve them with the greatest eagerness, he recommended his religious to show them ever the greatest deference, and to revere in their persons Jesus Christ Himself, the Sovereign Priest of God.

But he did more. One of his first ideas was to receive in his little sanctuary of adoration any priest who had one day or two which they could spend in recollection at the feet of Our Lord; knowing how difficult a long retreat often is to priests absorbed in the sacred ministry, not only on account of time and distance, but from the urgency of their functions.

But besides that, Blessed Eymard wished "to form an association of the priests of different parishes; to unite them by certain prayers, statutes, and periodical conferences, *and sanctify them by the Most Holy Sacrament.*" "These associates will live the Eucharistic life of Jesus Christ, which consists principally in the abnegation of self and the love of immolation. They will remember that their first duty is one of personal adoration *nos autem orationi instantes erimus* (Acts vi. 4); so that they may ensure by prayer the success of their ministry. And they will come down from the Eucharist like Moses from Mount Sinai, like the Apostles from the Last Supper, full of fire to announce His word and His glory *et ministerio verbi* (Acts vi. 4). They will bind themselves to maintain on all occasions the interests and the honor of Jesus Christ and to spread as far as possible the practice of daily visits before the tabernacle, and frequent Communion. In one word, in all their acts, in all their functions they will unite themselves to Jesus in the Blessed Eucharist, the eternal Priest, the model and grace of the sacerdotal order. But above all I should like to give priests the facility in their old age to spend the few remaining years of their lives at the feet of the Blessed Sacrament. Could there be a more honorable and pleasant retreat for veterans who have valiantly fought the battle of their Lord than one which would be offered to them at the feet of their King? There they could make a little halt before the great journey they have to take to eternity, and prepare themselves to appear before their Judge; and each would serve according to his strength. Those that were too infirm and sick would be tended lovingly by us as our fathers. They would visit the Blessed Sacrament from time to time to renew a life which old age and suffering had consumed. Those who could share in the adoration would do so. In vain has the devoted charity of certain persons striven to create houses of retreat for aged priests. These houses are almost always empty. Priests dread them; they seem like the threshold of the grave. A priest cannot bear the idea of remaining idle, isolated, alone with his own thoughts. But in a sanctuary filled with the solemnities of the Eucharistic service, round the altar of the Exposition, a priest would feel his piety always active. His charity is called forth; his zeal can still find its exercise. He is serving his apprenticeship for eternity. It would be a real heaven upon earth; a reward for the labors of his life, which have exhausted his physical strength without cooling the ardor of his soul." Such was the second work organized by Father Eymard. Our Lord alone can tell the hour of its full realization.

X

THE ARCHCONFRATERNITY OF THE MOST BLESSED SACRAMENT — THE PEOPLE'S EUCHARISTIC LEAGUE

Between the poor young workman condemned from childhood to labor beyond his strength, and the priest of God occupying, by his august character, his learning, and his virtues, the highest step of the social ladder, there is an innumerable company of faithful Christians, whom it was the third object of Blessed Eymard to enroll under the banner of the Blessed Sacrament by means of an aggregation or confraternity. "Enriched by His Holiness Pius IX with the most precious indulgences, this Archconfraternity of the Blessed Sacrament has for its main object to obtain for Our Lord in the Eucharist the greatest number of adorers in spirit and in truth. Filled with faith and love they adore Him on His throne, and unite themselves with our society in a fraternal union to promote the greatest glory of our King. Each associate shall promise to spend every month one hour before the Blessed Sacrament. This is the personal service: in addition to that he shall co-operate as far as possible in the work of the Altar Society, providing all things fitting for the tabernacle, and especially the lamps, needed in poor churches.

"It is also a duty for such associates to prepare a decent reception for our Lord when He deigns to visit the homes of His poor, and to accompany the priest who bears Him there, thus proclaiming their faith and love.

"The associates shall also attend the Benediction service whenever possible. In fact, whenever any homage is to be rendered to Our Lord in the Blessed Sacrament, there is the place of the associates. He is their King; they are His courtiers. That explains all."

Blessed Eymard had the consolation of seeing this plan of his carried out completely in Paris, Marseille, Angers, and Brussels, where the associates formed themselves into an important body, taking alternate weeks of Eucharistic service; and should other duties preclude the possibility of any one of the associates taking his turn of adoration, he offers a wax-taper before the throne of his King, which speaks of his devotion and love.

This is not enough. He surrounds the throne of Our Lord with the most beautiful flowers. Inanimate nature is made to sing the hosannah of the King of Love. And the eye, astonished at a beauty and profusion which brave all seasons and know no cessation, begins to see what is meant by a faith which understands, and a love which will serve, Jesus Christ.

Pharisees are not wanting who complain of this extravagance, and deplore the waste of what might be better employed.

"Jesus is King in the Blessed Sacrament," replied Blessed Eymard to such objectors. "He is a living King. Honor Him, then, with a living and royal service. A human king passes through the streets of a city. If no one cheers or salutes him, people ask, 'Can this be the king? No; it must be some stranger.' Now, here is Our Lord. Here is Our King. Where are the exterior and public homage due to His royalty?... Gifts to churches," he continued, "are the measure of the faith of a people. Faith lives in Italy, in Spain.... Jansenism has frozen it up in France; but it will revive! The faith which shuts itself up, and considers what is given to Our Lord as useless, is a leaven of Protestantism. It is quite true that we must give to the poor. But Jesus in the Blessed Sacrament is the first of the poor; and His suffering members will have the more abundant part if His share has been duly reserved.... To give to Jesus Christ, is it not an honor, a consolation, a want of our hearts? Certainly, every one cannot give presents to a king; unless one were intimate with a person of higher rank than oneself, would one dare even give him a nosegay for his feast? Well, Jesus is not like a human prince. He accepts the humblest homage—the widow's mite, the wild flower of the orphan child. What an honor!... And what a consolation for a loving heart to be able to say, 'I give to God directly of my economies, of my bread, of the fruit of my toil, of the sweat of my brow. I can share everything with Him, my Jesus!' Yes, without your offerings, without these waxlights, Jesus could not come out of His tabernacle. You put Him in the condition of a king. Say to Him, with loving confidence, 'You reign on a brilliant throne; it is our hearts which have raised it to You.'... Ah, may you often have the consolation of saying, 'I have given to Our Lord.'

"We must try to lift souls above and out of themselves; to give them, as a motive in the practice of virtue, the wish, the ambition to please Our Lord; to labor directly for Him, under Him, and with Him. Love is our life.

"*Trahit sua quemque voluptas.* Self-love makes men egotists; the love of the world, vicious; the love of God alone makes us good and happy.

"But all love must have an object. Jesus in the Blessed Sacrament is the sole end and aim of the adorer. One can certainly arrive at Christian perfection by the rigorous accomplishment of duty, by a life of perpetual struggle against self. But Jesus never said, 'Abide in penitence,' 'in humility,' or in any other virtue. No; this would be no center; the soul would be in prison. He said, 'Abide in My love. If you keep My commandments, you shall abide in My love; as I also have kept My Father's commandments, and do abide in His love' (John xv. 9, 10).

"God is love. To man, created in His image, love is also life; weakened, vitiated it may be, but capable of being brought back to its first principles. God comes to man through love, and love is the channel through which man returns to God. Man is incapable of attaching himself to God, save by His goodness and love. He fears His divine power; His Holiness shames the poor sinner in his fallen humanity. But the goodness of God! Ah, that is the thing which attracts us irresistibly. It binds us to Him, because we see God lowering Himself to the level of His creatures. It is only in His humiliations that we can dare to unite ourselves to Him, and in His voluntary abasement that we can call Him our brother, and ourselves His brethren, according to the flesh. He loves us; He gives Himself to us. Can we help loving Him, too?

"If we have to face a sacrifice," continues Blessed Eymard, "look at Our Lord, at least in thought. 'O my God, who hast so loved me, I wish to love Thee more than this sacrifice, than this privation, than this sorrow. And I will bear this trial, that I may give Thee back a portion of Thy love.' After an act like this, the sacrifice will cost you little or nothing; you will have already made it in your heart.

"It is all very well to say to Our Lord, 'My God, I love Thee with all my heart!' But love proves itself by deeds. Are you practicing His laws? Are you advancing in virtue? In that way I shall know if you are advancing in love. The first effect of the love of God in man is to make war against his self-love....

"But to live with Jesus we must be fed by Him. *Holy communion must be the pivot on which the life of an associate of the Blessed Sacrament turns.* Prepare yourself carefully for Holy Communion, for it is in Communion that you will enter into that law of love, and receive the needful grace; and to love truly, we must often receive Our Lord. Without that, we may know Him as Our Creator, as the Father of future glory, as a benefactor even; but we shall not love Him as a friend, with the familiarity of love. The Apostles had only received

Communion once, yet Jesus calls them His friends! What will He not, then, say to us who receive Him so often? Ah, go to Communion, then, if you wish to know the full sweetness of Our Lord—if you wish to know the extent of His love!

"Holy Communion should be the life of an associate, and all his actions preparations for, or thanksgivings after, it. In the morning he promises to keep all his good resolutions, in order to thank God for giving Himself to him; in the evening he makes his examination of conscience, and does his best to feel contrition for his faults, so as to be more worthy to receive Holy Communion the next morning. Each action is as a little flower which he hastens to offer Him before it fades. Thus his piety is a living thing; his heart is always turning towards Jesus. And this is life!

"He who rarely communicates preserves, perhaps, his share of grace for heaven. But how far off this heaven is! what faith it requires to look so far! The state of grace required for constant Communion is easy. It is for to-day, for to-morrow. One knows one must put on the 'wedding garment.' One tries to keep it pure and unsoiled, so as not to lose one's Communion.

"It is difficult to persevere in the pursuit of virtue; our nature is always reasserting itself. But in Holy Communion Jesus becomes part of ourselves, and forms Himself in us; so that we obtain courage and strength for the struggle. Holy Communion is as the mold in which Jesus forms our souls according to His will. He has said, 'He that eateth My flesh and drinketh My blood, liveth in Me, and I in him.'

"And how little it costs one to be humble when one has been to Holy Communion! Jesus has condescended to come down and dwell in us; is not that enough to annihilate all human pride?

"How easy, again, it is to be gentle under the influence of such tender goodness as that of Jesus!

"How dear our neighbor becomes to us when fed with the same Bread of Life, and loved with the same infinite love by Our Lord!

"Even the Cross loses its bitterness, for we feel in our hearts our Crucified Saviour.

"There are certain kinds of goodness which are not amiable or attractive to others. They are those which are formed by those continual struggles and sacrifices which a stern sense of duty imposes. Without Holy Communion, virtue may have a lion's strength; but without the Blood of the Lamb it cannot have His sweetness and tenderness. I firmly believe in the atmosphere of grace about the Blessed Sacrament, and the spots where it dwells. The Eucharist has a perfume which is felt even by the impious. So you, weeping mothers, wives, sisters, who are always asking for the conversion of one dearer to you than life, go to Communion. Bring back Jesus with you! It is a fire which, enkindled in your heart, will warm the hearts of those around you. Whether they will or not they will breathe the Blessed Eucharist. The sweetness and loving kindness which you have brought back from Holy Communion will react on your conduct, make you more patient, more gentle, and more forbearing; they will love you the better, without knowing it. And then He whom you bear in your breast, He will speak for you and touch their hearts. Oh, have faith in the influence of the presence of Jesus!

"You ask, 'What are the conditions of frequent Communion?' There is but one—*purity of life*. Jesus comes to us by reason of our purity.

"Are you in a state of grace? Do you hunger for Him? Come and feed on Him at once. Do not say, 'I have no merits. I am not fit.' That is no reason. You have nothing, it is true. Put yourself in the lowest place; but only wish ardently for Him.

"If not content with avoiding mortal sins, you strive to avoid venial ones, be sure that Jesus will receive you gladly. He will admit you into His Heart. No cobwebs will cover the entrance. He will accept your good-will in spite of all your imperfections. He will *dwell* with you; and then you will feel yourself, as it were, transformed; and you will say to Jesus, 'Take all. Reign in my heart. Enable me to love Thee always; and may I be Thy servant for all eternity.'

"The great comfort is, that Jesus accepts our *will*. If He only came to us in proportion to our good works, it would be fearful. What are the highest human virtues in presence of the holiness of God? But you are pure—at least you strive to be so. You love Him—at least you wish to do so. That is enough. Jesus will come to you with joy.

"Some souls are in constant fear. They have not a proper understanding of Holy Communion; We must forget our miseries, the infinite distance which separates us from God—and *think only of our need*. Our Lord calls us. He veils His holiness, His power, and only shows us His goodness, so that we may approach Him without fear. Remember also that the grace of preparation for Holy Communion is, above all, the grace of *confidence*—not even of self-examination or prayer. These things are good; but the true preparation is to have confidence in the words: 'Come; for I am the God of thy heart.' And this confidence honors God more than if you were to cast yourself upon the earth in a fit of despair. And if after Communion, you feel dry and without devotion, it is because you do not throw yourself enough upon the tender goodness, the intimate love of Our Lord. We feel as if He came to reproach us for our defects. But no. A friend does not come to see us to remind us of our shortcomings, and certainly does not begin by that. Let, then, Our Lord fill your heart. In Holy Communion He is all tenderness and love. The most solemn moment in the Christian life is the moment of thanksgiving. You have then at your disposal the King of heaven and earth, ready, with open hands, to fulfill all your wishes. Ask, then, freely—ask for all you need. Jesus is yours: make use of this gift. The Heavenly Father has given Him to you: learn how to take advantage of this inestimable mercy. The greater portion of us, alas, bury Him in ourselves. Ask, then, in His name. Pray in His name. Whatever God grants to you will have been paid for by a superabundant price. Jesus is worth more than every grace; and even if God were to give you heaven itself, it would still be less than His merits."

We will conclude these long extracts from Blessed Eymard's written or spoken words by one consoling thought. Some one said to him, "I wish to make a good Communion; but I have no special intention, I don't feel any particular need. I am afraid of abusing my permission to receive so frequently. I would rather wait and reserve myself for a more solemn occasion—a more pressing necessity." *"Oh,"* he replied, *"if you don't want to go to Communion for yourself, go to it for Jesus Christ.* To go to Communion for Him is to strive to console Him for the abandonment in which He is so often left by men. It is as if you told Him something of your sense of His infinite mercy for having given you this spiritual food. More than this, it is to give an occasion for the exercise of His love, of His ardent desire to give Himself to us, of His royalty to dispense His bounty.

"To go to Communion for Jesus Christ is to give Him, as it were, a new life, which He will consecrate to the glory of His Father. A pious Christian receives Him, unites himself to Him, becomes one of His members, and Jesus works and suffers in each. It is a wonderful corporation, wherein man acts and Jesus gives the grace; where man acquires merits and Jesus glorifies His Father. It is the body of love which Our Lord desired, and to perpetuate which He instituted the Blessed Sacrament. To refuse to go to Communion when one can—when Jesus Himself, by the mouth of His priest, permits one to do so—is simply to frustrate one of the fondest hopes of Our Lord. He knew us all in the Last Supper. He has reserved for each one of us our inheritance. He counts all our Communions, and gives commissions to His angels to bear these Hosts to us, consecrated by His almighty power and love. Do not leave Hosts untasted. Do not refuse the Divine messenger from the tabernacle, faithfully guarded by Peter and his successors. Let our Lord Jesus Christ bear fruit in you for your own salvation and the salvation of the whole world.

Adveniat regnum Tuum. May Thy Eucharistic reign be hastened, O Lord, in the hearts of all Thy servants."

XI

THE CONGREGATION OF THE BLESSED SACRAMENT APPROVED — THE SISTER-SERVANTS OF THE BLESSED SACRAMENT — THE CENACLE

"I wish to become a saint for the honor of my Master alone. I feel it will cost me many sacrifices. I will do what is right without glory, without honor, without affections, without success. All true vocations gained for Jesus Christ must cost me a living death, and yet no one shall perceive it. By suffering only shall I be able to serve the society of Our Lord."

Such was Blessed Eymard's resolve at the beginning of 1863; and his divine Master would not allow Himself to be outdone in generosity, and abundantly blessed the works of His faithful servant.

He had one ambition, and that was to see his little Society of the Blessed Sacrament canonically adopted by the Church. In that hope alone he placed its existence and its future prosperity. "Every branch which grows out of the trunk of Holy Church," he wrote, "grows and thrives. To remain, as it were, alongside of the trunk without being incorporated in it, is to condemn it to death. Our religious," he continued, "must profess for the Holy See the most absolute devotion and the most perfect submission, defending its primacy as the cause of Jesus Christ Himself, and maintaining all its rights and privileges, taking for the absolute law of their conduct its doctrines, its sentiments, and its good pleasure. The first hour of adoration each day shall be applied to the intentions of the Sovereign Pontiff; the second to those of the Ordinary, in whatever diocese we may be placed." We can, therefore, realize the extent of his joy when, on May 8, 1863, the Sovereign Pontiff, after having had the Society of the Blessed Sacrament, its rules, constitutions, objects, and results thoroughly examined by a congregation of Bishops and Regulars, solemnly approved and confirmed it. He received this decree of approbation, signed by Pius IX himself, on the 3rd of June following, at the hour of the first Vespers of Corpus Christi.

"Here we are at last," he exclaimed, in a transport of joy, "one of the family of Holy Church! The Pope is our first Superior, and canonical approbation has placed the society under its paternal tutelage. To be approved by the Pope, and by such a Pope! by Pius IX, who has done so much for the Church—the Pope of the Immaculate Conception—what a grace! What an honor for us! What an encouragement for the future!"

This approbation brought forth fruit. Blessed Eymard had the joy and consolation in the next few years of seeing an immense increase in the number of his religious members, and exposition of the Blessed Sacrament inaugurated in seven different towns in France.

On his return from Rome he sanctioned the formation of another branch of his work, for women to perpetuate the life of the Blessed Virgin after the Last Supper. These ladies were called "The Servants of the Most Holy Sacrament." Their name explains their object. They serve the Blessed Eucharist, through love, in prayer and immolation at His feet; and their spirit is the same as that of the priests of their order, *"to exalt Our Lord and annihilate themselves."*

One thing which Blessed Eymard ardently desired was not granted to him in life; but we feel sure it will some day be fulfilled. It was the restoration of the place where the "Last Supper" was held. "Is it possible," he exclaimed one day, "that the first room which held the Adorable Sacrament should be in the power of the infidels? That in the august sanctuary where Jesus consummated the greatest act of His love, in which His Apostles listened to His last words, and wherein, after His Ascension, the Holy Ghost descended upon them—that in this sanctuary Mahomet should reign! Ah, who will give me the means to buy back this most sacred spot, and therein to expose once more Our Lord Jesus Christ? If ever that day comes, with only a stick in my hand, I will go throughout all Europe begging for means to raise a magnificent basilica over the 'upper room' of the Last Supper."

XII

HIS LONG RETREAT AT ROME — PERSONAL SANCTIFICATION

In 1865 Blessed Eymard had to return to Rome on important business. He was detained a long time. The piety and faith of the Roman people delighted him. He called Rome "the city of the most Holy Sacrament," and never failed assisting at the Forty Hours' adoration, which exists in Rome throughout the whole year in the different Churches. He took advantage of the leisure he had there to make a month's retreat. Alone with God, he examines, scrutinizes his most secret thoughts. He hunts out what he has still to sacrifice, and shakes off the least speck of human dust.

"In all things," he writes in his notes, "I will ask myself this question: What has there been for *God alone* in this or that action? in this or that thought? I see that I have often given myself to our Lord in the Blessed Sacrament from zeal for His exterior glory. My activity has been for outside things—miserably lax when concentrated within." Our Lord tries him by withdrawing all sensible consolation. He complains lovingly: "I who am generally so sensitive, who can cry so easily, I find myself cold, dry, and insensible. My God, I know I do not deserve to shed tears of love, nor even of sorrow and penitence, in Thy sight! A dry sorrow—that is the only portion of humbled pride of a heart that has loved itself too much.... I will try and understand what that love of Our Lord is which has made Him bear with me so long and so patiently. When my self-love has been crushed by the sight, perhaps the ice will melt." A few days later he writes: "At last I see my way. It is only by absolute mortification of the will within and without that I shall arrive at Our Lord. This spirit, which despoils me of myself, will graft Jesus in me and inoculate me with His life and His virtues. Like St Paul 'I fill up those things that are wanting of the sufferings of Christ' (Coloss. i. 24). This is the death-blow to nature. With my senses I will act with the hardness of a master—as one treats a slave always on the point of revolting from the yoke. My body can only be tamed by blows. Reason with it, and it does not listen; without corporal mortification it is useless to strive. That is a heresy which, in these days, has invaded the robust piety of our ancestors, and especially in the spiritual direction of souls. 'One must guide them by gentleness,' they say. But you put them to sleep! True love crucifies. All love that does not lead to sacrifice is only a disguised egotism.

"The next rule is to treat my soul with patience. My mind is frivolous, ignorant. I must guide it like a little child; not roughly, but gently; bring it back, but without violence, and humble myself more and more at having such a miserable spirit incapable of any fixity in the things of God.

"As regards my heart, I must lead it by the way of sacrifice. Our hearts are so strong! They are the very depth of man. How gladly do we make creatures the centers of our rest! But we must tear away our idols resolutely, and then, being free from all human ties, we shall show ourselves unreservedly at Our Lord's feet. *Fecisti nos ad Te, Deus!*

"If we shrink from this, if we look back, beware! It is a despisal of God. If we try and divide our affections, Our Lord will always have the smallest share. Take, then, my whole heart, O my God! After all, it is not so large!

"In a fight there must be two parties. If Jesus be not in me, who will help me to fight against the 'old man' in my breast? To put no hindrance in the way of the growth of Jesus in my heart, that must be my main object. That is the path in which Our Lord leads me. To form Jesus in me, to make Him my strength, my center—that must be my sole aim."

And Our Lord attracted him so strongly that everything outside of His Presence tired him to death. We find this note among his papers:

"A poor, miserable day, all spent in visits and in letter-writing. My soul feels quite dried up. I feel that an ounce of quiet recollection is worth more than a hundred pounds of exterior work." Another time to write this one word— *"Cattivo!"* (Bad).

"The way to love Our Lord *is* to love Him," writes St Francis of Sales. So Blessed Eymard writes: "The way to unite ourselves to Our Lord is to *be* united. Of what use are subtle reasonings? The simple thing is to place yourself in His hands and follow His inspirations. It is the secret of Our Lord's words, 'Abide in My Love' (John xv. 9). How unhappy I am when I am alone! The Divine Heart of Jesus is my element, as the ocean to the fish, the air to the being who breathes. When Jesus has not been with me during the day, when I have rested in my work, or in that of others, I feel, 'What have I done? Nothing, or worse than nothing. I have spoiled all.' I must then be united to Our Lord, as the human nature of Christ was united to the Person of the Word. On this condition alone a Christian becomes a member of His Body. The law of this union, this total dependence on Our Lord, is 'Nothing for me, nothing by me.' Henceforth I cannot receive either honor or affection, or any earthly good; because to be honored or loved, or possess anything, one must be somebody, and I am now only a thing molded by the will of Our Lord. Oh, how is it that I have so long neglected such a powerful means of grace? What merits I have lost! What barren actions without fruit! By a closer union with Jesus Christ my actions, my sufferings would have acquired a priceless value. Jesus would have labored and merited, and the Eternal Father would have looked complacently on His well-beloved Son in me.

"I will, then, renew the gift of my personality to Our Lord as often as I draw breath," he continues. "Grant me, O my God, the gift of strength. It is needful for me in the warfare I have undertaken for Thy love. I do not wish to be wise, nor virtuous, nor learned, nor eloquent. I wish only for one thing—the strength to live for Thee, to serve Thee, to be nourished by Thy love—by that pure love which was that of Jesus at the moment of His Incarnation, and which immolated the human Self of the Son of Mary in the Divine Self of the Son of God."

The Father ends his retreat by offering it thus to Our Lord:

"O Lord Jesus, I sacrifice to Thee my whole personality without reserve or condition. What I wish to be is simply a servant living in his Master's house, always at His orders and at His disposal, flying to obey Him joyfully and gladly, and only caring for that which pleases most His adorable Majesty."

XIII

MODESTY, HUMILITY AND KINDNESS

"I do not seek to be eminent in virtue for myself," Blessed Eymard writes; "but my service requires that I should do everything in the most perfect manner, and especially that I should acquire such virtues as are most pleasing to, and most in sympathy with, the Heart of Jesus. First, then, modesty, which is as the etiquette of the royal service of the Eucharist; then humility, sweetness, bearing patiently with others; little virtues, which, like violets, thrive best in the shade, are nourished with dew, and which, though not making any show, do not fail to spread a sweet smell. Our Lord was the essence of modesty; His life was a perfect pattern of it. The Christians in the first centuries looked upon this virtue as one of his distinctive characteristics, and St Paul exhorts them 'by the modesty of Christ' (2 Cor. x. 1). It is a quality equally dear to the heart of Mary. It should be the distinguishing characteristic of the servant of the Blessed Eucharist. Interiorly, modesty honors Our Master, preserving us, in a religious respect, at His feet; exteriorly, it exercises us in all virtues, for it is a constant mortification of the senses. It makes our tongues loving and charitable, our looks pure, our appetites temperate; it involves, likewise, the constant practice of humility.

"The way to acquire it, and to keep it, is to live continually in the presence of Jesus, remembering that His eye is always watching us.

"How few people have I found, even among pious persons and

religious, who were thoroughly modest *tête-à-tête!* Modesty in the streets is easy enough; one fears scandal. But to maintain modesty on every occasion in private life is difficult, because it is the immolation of naturalism in our daily intercourse. To be thoroughly modest, one must be supernatural with everybody."

Blessed Eymard possessed this virtue in an eminent degree. By dint of constant watchfulness and hard fights, it had become a second nature to him. Even in speaking to others, it was remarked that he rarely seated himself very close to them, or looked them in the face; but generally fixed his eyes on some pious picture, though without any effort or affectation. Every one felt that his presence inspired respect and a certain reserve; his very look made one recollected. He used to say to his young priests, "Become shy. I was given that advice when I was only eighteen by the General of the Chartreux; I have never forgotten it, and it has been very useful to me."

One day he was reproached for not having recognized an intimate friend who had passed him. He said simply, "I am very sorry; but I never saw him. In the street I never look at any one closely enough to distinguish one from the other."

"Chastity," he would say, "is the crown of modesty. By it one becomes the friend of the King—'He that loveth cleanness of heart shall have the King for his friend' (Prov. xxii. 11). Jesus, then, loves in us Mary, His Mother, the purest of all virgins.... To be humble is to love Jesus Christ in His humiliations. It is to receive from God, with thorough submission of heart, the humiliations which fall to our lot, and to look upon them as a blessing. It is to accept our state and its duties, and not to blush at our condition. If I love Jesus, I ought to be like Him, love what He loved, do what He did, what He preferred above everything.... How easy this humility of heart is! It is only a question of imitating Our Lord Jesus Christ and of loving Him. Our Lord does not ask us to love humility for its own sake; but to love Jesus in His humiliations.... 'The sacrifice,' you will say, 'is the same.' Yes; but sacrifice for the sake of sacrifice alone is difficult; for one whom we love, it becomes light—witness the mother who immolates herself habitually for the child of her love. The humility to which we must aspire is not that alone which consists in transferring to God all the honor of success, and which we can practice in the time of abundance and prosperity; but when assailed by temptations, by interior storms which overwhelm both heart and mind, by outward trials which threaten the very existence of our most cherished works, if then we can say to God, 'My Lord, I thank Thee! I deserve all this, and give Thee thanks that I am not fallen even lower,'—that is true humility, the humility of our Saviour and His saints."

Blessed Eymard's humility was of this stamp; but he wanted every one to forget that he was humble. He appeared to accept man's praises; but would say afterward to his intimates: "When I am praised I feel that I am being insulted, or that they are laughing at me. But I would rather receive praise in silence, than protest. How many, while protesting humility, do it in reality to place crowns on their own heads!"

"Humility begets gentleness, sweetness. He who knows what he is, is gentle with his neighbor, gentle and patient with himself. If he is tried, he knows that he deserves nothing else. The contrarieties, the vexations of others are only, after all, God's instruments. As for himself, he knows what he is at bottom; and without murmuring against his miseries, he bears them with patience, as the poor man does his rags, or as the little child allows its weakness, knowing its mother's heart. To become gentle, I shall not try and reason with myself, nor struggle too much against my nature, nor arouse myself to penance or vengeance against myself. All this is too militant, and would awake feelings the reverse of gentle. But I will look upon Jesus, in His sweetness and gentleness and meekness. I will think of His wish that I too should be meek and gentle, loving and humble. In Jesus all is love and light.

"But especially I will contemplate the Holy Eucharist. I will eat of this divine manna, and thus every morning make my provision of sweetness for the day. In the Heart of Jesus there is no indignation, no desires of vengeance towards His enemies. He is all tenderness and compassion. He is gentle by nature, gentle by His mission. The little child, the grievous sinner, do not fear the Saviour; the poor, the little ones in this world, all love Jesus. But, besides all this, it is my duty to be gentle and meek. Am I not the servant of the servants of God? Of what use is severity? or harsh and cutting words? It is Our Lord who is Master."

This was the keynote of his life as Superior. "Let others be fathers," he would say. "As for me, I only aspire to be your mother. It is the custom of little minds, the moment they see a fault, to wish to correct it. As for me, I prefer waiting till Our Lord Himself makes the person conscious of the defect: *then* I speak or act. Otherwise, it is I who see what is wrong, and not the person who is to amend it. Of what use is it to go before grace? or to flatter myself that I am wiser than Our Lord by wanting to do that for which He has not yet found the fitting time?"

Such was Blessed Eymard. Loving, gentle, humble, modest; but with a goodness which had no limit; a gentleness which never varied; a humility which was as genuine as it was attractive; a modesty without stiffness. Such were the fruits of that "death in Jesus Christ," of which he was always speaking; such the perfumes with which he daily embalmed Our Lord's Body in the Blessed Eucharist.

XIV

TRIALS

But Blessed Eymard's earthly course was nearly run. Only two years more, and Our Lord would reward his loyal services. But before, he was to be still further tried in the furnace of tribulation; he was to be polished with the diamond of sorrow. Our Lord loved him too much not to give him that finishing touch which only suffering imparts.

First, he was filled with a sort of imperious longing to fly from the world and from men, and from all the miseries which he had continually before his eyes. But the Master ordered him, at his peril, to stick to his post.

The burden of souls, the responsibility of his numerous religious family, overpowered him. He judged himself as utterly incapable of bearing so heavy a burden, and implored his spiritual children to let him lay it down. "If you love me," he wrote to them, "you would rejoice at my leaving you. For eight years I have fought and struggled; my mission now is at an end. The society, approved by Rome, prospers and thrives. I sigh after solitude, silence, and the hidden life of Jesus Christ in the Blessed Sacrament. Oh, how sweet it would be to devote myself, under obedience, to the welfare of this dear society as the last and humblest of its subjects! I hope to obtain from your charity and true friendship, this inestimable boon." But his children would not hear of it. Unanimously they re-elect him as Superior. He accepted the post with tears. "My God!" he exclaimed, "if it were not for Thy glory and Thy will, I would fly and hide myself anywhere under Thy feet. But Thou willest that I should suffer all these human miseries; that I should live amongst them—with them.... Amen! At least I will strive to glorify Thee by patience, gentleness, humiliation, the loss of my own liberty, abnegation of myself. But in the midst of all this, grant me to see Thy face; grant me peace of heart, union with Thee, and love of my neighbor. My God, may Thy name be for ever blessed! I will serve Thee as the orderly of a king. An orderly has no proper name, no personal authority, no particular honor; he is only a servant—*minister Christi!*"

But Our Lord was pleased to overwhelm him soon after with cares and anxieties. All, at His hand, was well and wisely ordered; but He made him taste of His own cup of dereliction. He deprived him of His presence—of all sensible consolation. And the poor father, who, until now, had found in his adoration a peace and a consolation which comforted him in all his other sorrows, burst forth in these touching words of complaint: "Alas, I am deprived of God! Formerly a quarter of an hour at the feet of the Blessed Sacrament brought calm and sunshine to my soul. Now whole hours leave me desolate!"

But he was not alone to feel abandoned by God. Friendship both valuable and precious to him were suddenly and unaccountably snapped; in fact, his best friends deserted him; while he was overwhelmed with the bitterest calumnies and misrepresentations.

At the same time, Our Lord, as it were, revealed to him all the horrors of which Paris is the focus and the center; and this knowledge filled him not only with sorrow, but with fear.

One day a venerable priest came to him with a little case containing a number of consecrated Hosts. He had received them from an unhappy Freemason, a member of a secret society, who had profaned a tabernacle, but had enough sense of religion left not to dare throw the precious particles into a drain, as his accomplices had done. He had kept them more than ten years. At last remorse conquered shame, and he went and owned his crime to one of God's ministers.

No words can express the grief of Blessed Eymard when this sad story was revealed to him. He felt it almost as a death-blow. During two nights these Hosts were exposed in reparation; and he passed nearly the whole of that time on his knees at the feet of the Master so shamefully outraged by His creatures. Writing to a friend, he says "This business has made me quite ill. I don't feel as if I could bear it."

Now and then he had a presentiment of his approaching death. It consoled, yet made him anxious at the same time. "I have still so much to do!" he would say. "Beg of Our Lord to give me a little more time—they rob me of it. I have scarcely a moment to myself."

This was quite true. People came to him at every hour of the day; his very instants were counted and quarreled for. But he was at every one's beck and call. A friend one day said to him, "Why not have certain fixed hours for the parlor and for confession? it would save your strength. But then you must be firm, and positively refuse to see anyone except at those times." He thought a moment, and then replied, "But Our Lord has no fixed hours. He is always at hand, even waiting. If I were to follow your advice, I should be no longer a servant. As our Lord always receives everybody, His servants must be always there to answer in His name. Besides," he added, "Our Lord knows very well what He makes me do. I am not at task-work; I am a day-laborer!" "But you are worried to death by trifles." "What I think trifles are very often important to those who come and consult me," he replied; "or, at least, they think so, which comes to the same thing. Would you rob me of the merit of patience?"

We shall not exaggerate if we say that, during these last years, the Cross was his daily bread. He acknowledged this: "Our good God loves us well!" he exclaimed one day; "for it is by the Cross that He rewards His friends. St John had preached and toiled and served Him faithfully; yet Our Lord allowed Herod to decapitate him; and he never uttered a word of complaint. As for us, the Cross, certainly, does not fail us;... but it is a good sign. And each morning I say to Our Lord, 'What fresh blow will fall on me to-day?' I mean *blows;* for, as for crosses, they are not worth speaking about."

But all this was as nothing as compared to the interior troubles which at that time Our Lord permitted to test the faith and love of His faithful servant. We should have known little of them had not Blessed Eymard, unconsciously, described them himself in an instruction he gave "on the true love of God." It was impossible to mistake the expression of intense suffering on his face, or fail to see that he was speaking from his own experience. He said:

"There is a love which loves God for Himself, and only finds its exercise in what costs him most sacrifice and self-chosen suffering, which are the essence of real love. But God, as it were, persecutes the soul which loves Him like that. It is a hard matter! He immolates His very self; and as there is always the temptation to seek oneself, God fights with the soul, and the struggle is torture. He annuls the intellect; He stifles even the heart. He plunges the soul into darkness, into temptations against faith, against even the goodness of God; and so all peace is at an end. A director can do nothing in such a case. One trembles for the present; the past fills one with terror; to the future one dare not look. What, then, is to be done? *Accept all.* Our Lord wills to leave you in that state, for which you are not accountable. He waits till you say, 'Lord, do with me what Thou willest! It is by Thy will that I am thus tormented, therefore I will wish for it too. Instead of offering Thee good deeds, or holy works, I will offer Thee my miseries which Thou hast shown me.' But, above all, do not examine yourself too narrowly. If you do at such a time you will go mad! God wishes to prove you, to see if you love Him better than your will, even should that be supernatural. Be quiet—bide His time. You will glorify Him even in this, your hell!... And your heart, which, so short a time ago, was in paradise, is now as cold as ice, and torn to pieces with conflicting thoughts. To say, 'I love Thee,' seems a blasphemy. You feel no love at all.... Never mind. Say to Our Lord, 'When Thou didst let me feel Thy sweetness, I was very happy! Now I am in a desert, and without water. Well, I will love Thee more than when I reveled in the sweetness of Thy love. 'My heart is dead, and says it cannot love Thee. Well, I will love Thee in spite of my heart—*by my will!*' These terrible struggles are sent to every soul which strives to be united to Him. This union with God must be soldered with fire!"

During the year which preceded his death, Blessed Eymard was also tried in the furnace of physical pain, which only left him when he was ripe for heaven. Rheumatic gout seized hold of him in the most acute form, causing intense suffering, paralyzing first one member, then another, and not sparing any part of his body. Yet his sweetness and cheerfulness never deserted him. "This is what I call an admirably disposed disease," he said one day, smiling. "It makes very little show, but gives one great suffering. So one has less pity from people round one; and Our Lord has it all."

This illness was, in fact, the crowning point of his patience. It would be impossible to find a patient so amiable, so easy to nurse, as this good father. The violent neuralgic attacks which he had suffered from all through his life, more or less, now came back to him, in his enfeebled state, with increased violence. A bad night, or an increase of anxiety, or some slight sorrow was enough to bring them on. During these terrible crises of pain, stretched on his bed, the poor father was as incapable of speaking a word as of making a movement. The least ray of light, the smallest sound, redoubled his sufferings; but he would make super-human efforts to overcome the agony, so as to be loving and gentle towards those who came to him. After a very bad night, one of his priests said to him, "Ah, Father, I fear you will have one of your attacks of neuralgia again to-day." "Well," he replied, smiling, "if Our Lord sends it, it shall be welcome." In spite of this state of continual suffering he regularly fulfilled his duty of adoration, and preached Eucharistic doctrine to the large congregation in his Paris sanctuary whenever a Sunday or a feast-day brought many together. To die on his *prie-dieu* was the object of his ambition. But Our Lord refused him this consolation. The disciple had to drink of the chalice of his Master to the dregs.

But this vigorous tree was to bear one more fruit in the autumn before it was laid low.

XV

OUR LADY OF THE MOST BLESSED SACRAMENT

On the 1st of May, 1868, being at Saint-Maurice, a little country house which he had taken, far away from the noise and bustle of Paris, to be, as he expressed it, "a little paradise for such of the members of the Adoration as Our Lord called to a more contemplative life," Blessed Eymard opened the Exercises for the month of Mary. He closed a beautiful allocution on our duties towards this good Mother with the following words:

"Well, let us honor Mary under the title of 'Our Lady of the Most Holy Sacrament.' Yes, let us say with confidence and love, 'Our Lady of the Most Holy Sacrament, Mother and Model for all adorers, pray for us who have recourse to you!'"

He was radiant; his voice trembled with emotion. He felt as if he had been able thus to pay a debt of gratitude to her who had first led him to the tabernacle, and who had sustained and encouraged him with such maternal solicitude in the first foundation of his society. "Our Lady of the Blessed Sacrament—it is only a new name for an ancient truth," he would say. "We revere, with reason, all the mysteries in the life of the Mother of God. Contemplative and domestic souls have found an example in her existence in Nazareth; broken hearts; consolation in Our Lady of Dolors; great sacrifices; strength, with her, at the foot of the Cross. Well, Mary lived fifteen years after the Ascension of her Divine Son. How did she spend those weary days of exile? What fresh grace may be gathered from this important part of her life? The Book of Acts seems to tell us clearly enough. The first Christians, it is there said, lived in union and peace, in the most ardent charity, sighing for martyrdom, and to prepare themselves worthily for it, persevering in the 'breaking of bread'—(Acts ii. 42).

"Living on and by the Eucharist, gathering round the tabernacle to pray and sing spiritual canticles, such was the distinctive character of the primitive Church as recorded by St Luke; such also was the *résumé* of the last years of the Blessed Virgin, who found in the adorable Host, the blessed Fruit of her womb, and in the life of union with Our Lord in His tabernacle, the happy times of Bethlehem and Nazareth. Yes, it was Mary, above all others, who persevered in the 'breaking of bread.' Eucharistic souls, who wish to live only for the Blessed Sacrament, who have made the Eucharist your center and His service your only work, Mary is your model, her life your grace. Only persevere with her in the 'breaking of bread.'...

Our Lord," he continued, "having given us Mary for our mother, we must honor and love her as her children. But to enter into the spirit of our vocation, and make all tend towards that one end, we must study and strive to imitate the life of Mary in the upper chamber, and her devotion to the service—love of the Blessed Sacrament. Mary stood on the mount of Calvary to die there with Jesus. She came down with the beloved disciple, the son of her adoption, and recommenced her maternity at the feet of the Sacred Host.

"Oh, do not fear, if you are the elect of the Blessed Eucharist; it is to Mary that you owe it. It is she who has led you by the hand to our Saviour's feet. Put yourself under her direction; and to become faithful servants of your King, Jesus, be devout children to Mary, who is the mother of Our Lord's servants. She is the only perfect imitator of the virtues of her Divine Son. She has the secret of His love. Her great mission is to form Jesus in us. It is a mother's part to train and educate her children. It seems as if, when He was dying, Jesus said to Mary, 'I bequeath into your hands the fruit of My redemption, the salvation of men, the service of the Sacrament of My Love. Form, for Me, adorers in spirit and in truth, who shall serve Me and adore Me as you have done.' In your communications with Jesus, therefore, think of Mary. Try to speak as she would have done; imitate her habits; act as she did; share in her love and in her sufferings, and all in Mary will say to you, 'Jesus, what can I do for the better serving of Jesus, for the greater glory of Jesus?' The life of Mary in the *cenaculum* should be the type of yours. Throw yourself on your knees by her side; adore with her. What a profound, interior, intimate adoration was hers! Everything in Mary lost itself, and was absorbed in her Son. A current of grace united the Heart of Jesus in the Host with the heart of Mary the adorer. Two flames mingled in one fire—a fire of glory and of love. God was perfectly adored by His Mother, who was His creation.... What a joy to Jesus when He received that homage from His Divine Mother! How happy He must have felt at having for her consolation left her His Sacramental Presence! I believe that He would have instituted the Blessed Eucharist for Mary only....

"When you go to Holy Communion," added Blessed Eymard, "strive to unite yourself to her wishes, and go to Communion with her faith and love. Is it not the custom for mothers to adorn and beautify, even with her own ornaments the child who is about to be led to the nuptial altar? At Cana did not Mary spare the confusion of the newly-married couple, and throw the cloak of her Son's power over their indigence? Oh, yes, the best preparation for Holy Communion is that which is made by Mary; and Jesus will come to you far more willingly if He sees in you the faithful imitators of His Holy Mother. Mary, in the supper-room, must likewise have looked after all things necessary for the Holy Sacrifice. Can we not fancy her making the linen with holy, skillful hands? When you, too, are working for the worship of the Eucharist, unite your intention to the joy of your Mother, working for her Son in His Sacramental Presence, as formerly she worked for Him as an infant. This thought will make you happy....

"The intimate knowledge of Our Lord which belonged to the Blessed Virgin, more penetrating than that of the seraphim or cherubim, gave her a perfect acquaintance with the Heart of Jesus; and therefore she understood, better than any human or angelic creature, the immensity of the gift of the Eucharist. She knew all the sacrifices of Jesus, and the struggles it had cost His Soul when He instituted this Divine Sacrament; just as she knew His anguish in the Garden of Olives. She foresaw all that her Divine Son would have to drink of ignominy and outrage in order to perpetuate His Presence in the midst of ungrateful men. When Jesus, before the Last Supper, announced to Mary that the hour was come for the triumph of His love; that He was about to institute the Adorable Sacrament, by means of which all Christians throughout all countries could partake of the happiness of union with Him, and become in Holy Communion one with their Saviour and their God,—Mary adored in deepest gratitude.... She consented to put off the hour of her reward and to remain on earth, to guard and serve the Blessed Eucharist, and to teach other Christians to guard, to love, and to adore this Sacrament of Love. What a mother! What a model! Happy were the disciples who could adore beside Mary, and learn from her august mouth how to serve their Saviour Jesus!"

This is the last tribute of Blessed Eymard to the glory of the Blessed Eucharist. Mary hastened to crown the devoted child who had inscribed the name of "Our Lady of the Blessed Sacrament," at the close of his life, on the altar dedicated to her.

XVI

DEATH OF BLESSED EYMARD

"Our Lord shows such delicate consideration for me that the end must be near at hand," wrote Blessed Eymard to a friend about this time. He felt that, from the excessive purity of intention demanded of him, his Divine Master was initiating him into the heavenly life, where nothing soiled can enter. He went into retreat, and there, under the conduct of Our Lady of the Blessed Sacrament, in silence with Jesus, he cast an earnest look on his soul, and purified it more and more before submitting it to the rigorous examination of the just judge.

To hear his self-accusations, and the way he laid bare the secret folds of his human self, one might fancy indeed that a ray of the holiness of God had darted into his soul; and he trembled.

"I feel that Our Lord cannot be satisfied with me—that I have neglected His glory and His grace—that I am an unfaithful, unprofitable servant. But, O my God, as you allow me to tell you all my misery, it is to pardon me. As you permit me still to pray, it is that I shall be heard. Blessed be the Lord God, who hath not turned away the eyes of His mercy from His erring and miserable servant.... What is the cause of the little progress I have made? It is because I have served God mainly in His glory. I have not embraced ardently and resolutely the humility of Jesus Christ. I have wanted to be somebody through Him and with Him. This is the last word of the old man in me. O Mary, who first brought me to Jesus, lead me back again to His feet."

Going carefully into an examination of his affections, truth compels him to give God the glory for one thing. "My heart has always belonged to Jesus in the Host. No one has ever possessed that poor heart of mine, save my Master." The root of the evil is elsewhere, in that self which cannot make up its mind to die, and struggles ever to regain that life which must be annihilated.

"Ah, if my soul be languid, it is my self-love which tires it, which runs after apparent good, and would act of itself without God. War, then, to the death to this self-seeking—to this human life in me. The way to gain the victory is to reject all idea of independence, and to force myself never to retard or go before the hour of the will of God; no, not by one minute. I must live in entire and direct dependence on Our Lord. O my Jesus, Thou art the truth, the way and the life. Thou shalt be the law of my will, the criterion of my examinations. When Thou art silent, I will wait for a sign from Thee. I will labor without any over-anxiety; not troubled by failure, not seeking for success. I am only a *day-laborer* in God's vineyard." These last words are the summary of his life. He had placed himself unreservedly in the hands of God, trusting in His mercy and goodness; and spent his days in the service of his Master, without regretting their close or wishing for the morrow. He is at peace, for he is in the hands of God. But the hour of eternity is about to strike for him, and he knows it, though he does not wish other people to pay any attention to it. He will labor and serve till the last hour of his life.

But the anxiety of those around him insists on his taking a little rest, and at last he yields to their reiterated entreaties. He is advised to breathe once more his native air, and to renew his strength amidst the mountains where he had passed his childhood and youth. But for him there was another attraction—the thought of seeing again the sanctuary of Notre-Dame du Laus. "Laus!" he exclaimed, "Laus! Oh, how I long to see it again! Our Lady showered such special graces upon me there. I can see now the pillar where I leant crying so bitterly over my sins after a general confession. What a happiness it would be to me to be there once more alone, and to be able to pray there quietly as long as I pleased!"

He left Paris on the 17th of July. The day before was Thursday. He had determined to preach once more, but it was necessary to warn him when the hour for the sermon drew near. All day he had been nailed to his chair by violent rheumatic pains. But he would make the effort, and surpassed himself. His last words were, "Yes, we believe in the love which God has for us (1 John iv. 16). Believe in the love. All is there. It is not enough to believe in the truth; we must believe in the love; and the expression of that love is Our Lord Jesus Christ in the Most Blessed Sacrament. This is the faith which loves Our Lord. Ask for it; ask for this pure and simple faith from the Holy Eucharist. Men may teach us; but Our Lord alone can give us the grace to believe in Him and to love Him. Come and communicate; to acquire, not sensible consolation, but the strength of faith. The Eucharist is there! What do you want more?"

On the 22nd of July he celebrated the Holy Sacrifice in the sanctuary of Our Lady of La Salette, near Grenoble. That tender Mother, who, on that very day thirty-three years before, had filled the heart of the young priest with ineffable consolations while offering his first Sacrifice, came to sustain his sinking arm at the moment when he consecrated for the last time the adorable Victim. He could not finish his thanksgiving but feeling a little better in the afternoon he resumed his journey, being most anxious to return to his old home at La Mure. During the drive, however, he was seized with a kind of congestion of the brain; half his head and body were paralyzed, and when he arrived he could not speak a word, but fell into the arms of his devoted sister, whom God rewarded for her lifelong devotion to her brother by permitting her to be with him, and by bringing him back to her in these his last moments. The disease gained ground rapidly; that exhausted nature, worn out far beyond its strength, had no power of resistance; and the most dangerous symptom in the case arose from his extreme weakness. Perfectly calm in the midst of his sufferings, unable to speak, but replacing by a tender smile the loving words of which he alone had the secret, he drew gently nearer and nearer to his end. He knew the bad opinion of the doctors, and he accepted gratefully the many prayers and vows offered for his recovery. But he himself was perfectly indifferent, willing either to live or die, and leaving both to the good pleasure of his Lord and Master.

The only sorrow he seemed to feel was that he was dying far away from his spiritual children, whom he had brought forth with such pain and labor, and whose training had cost him such incalculable sacrifices. But the Master exacted this last sacrifice from His devoted servant, and his religious had the inexpressible sorrow of hearing of the death of their much-loved father and founder almost as soon as they had received the news of his serious illness.

As for himself, his only surprise was that any one should hasten to his bedside. "Why did you come?" he asked of two of his priests who had hastened from Paris at the first note of alarm. "It wasn't worth while!" He had recovered the use of his speech; and dying was, in his eyes, but the accomplishment of his service; a necessary act to be got over as quickly as possible.

Twice he had the consolation of assisting at the Holy Sacrifice, which was offered up in his bedroom. And the last day he received again in the morning Our Lord in Holy Viaticum. He had been administered the night before, and received Extreme Unction. When that was over he turned to his sister, and said, "Good-bye, dear sister. It is finished." Fifteen hours later he expired peacefully, without any agony or struggle, fixing his eyes with an expression of hope and joy on the image of his crucified Saviour.

His face took then an unaccustomed brightness, like the reflection of the life of the blessed. The sweetest smile hovered on his lips, his eyes were gently open, and he seemed to answer the sobs of those who surrounded him by those familiar words of his, "Whether I am here or not, what on earth does it signify? Have you not the Blessed Eucharist always with you?"

Our Lord called Blessed Eymard to Himself on Saturday, the 1st of August, the day of the feast of St Peter's Chains, and at the hour when the first Vespers were being sung for the feast of the Portiuncula, at the age of fifty-seven years, five months and twenty-seven days.

His body, dressed in his sacerdotal vestments, and with the alb in which, twelve years before, he had made the first exposition of the Blessed Sacrament, remained uncovered till the Sunday evening. Two persons scarcely sufficed during that time to answer to the needs of the faithful who crowded round the coffin, anxious to touch the body with different pious objects. The priests of the neighborhood vied with one another for the honor of bearing his loved remains to their last resting-place. The Dean of La Mure gave the absolutions amidst a dense crowd, all deeply moved, and many of whom the Church could not hold. It was with the utmost difficulty that the clergy and procession could make their way through the crowd, all of whom were struggling to get one more sight of the beautiful, calm, and even radiant face which was about to be covered for ever from their earthly sight.

A *prie-dieu* of stone covered his tomb. He was buried beside the Church, his face turned towards the altar; he was at two steps from that holy tabernacle, whence Jesus, speaking to his heart for the first time, conquered him to His service for ever.

In 1877 his precious remains were transferred to Paris and placed under the sanctuary of his church, at the foot of the Throne of Perpetual Exposition. Thus was realized his life-long wish: "Reign, O Lord Jesus, reign in my heart and in the hearts of all men. *May I, by the total annihilation of myself, become a footstool for Thy Eucharistic Throne.*"

XVII

THE PROCESS OF BEATIFICATION

When Pierre-Julien Eymard was called to God, he left as a pledge of life to his Congregation, as yet in its infancy, rules full of his spirit and the example of his admirable virtues, especially his incomparable faith in the living Presence of Jesus Christ in the Host, and an ardent zeal for the glorification of this Adorable Master. Nevertheless, although his first sons were thoroughly convinced of the sanctity of their Founder, as documents written the day after his death testify, they did not think of taking the steps necessary for the presentation of a Cause of Beatification to the Roman Curia. Moreover, the terrible war of 1870 soon broke out, followed by the revolution and the tyrannical government of the Commune. Ten years later, the laws expelling all religious Congregations from France, placed the Institute in great danger, by closing its houses at Paris, Marseille, Angers, Arras, and St Maurice of Versailles. Fortunately, the house at Brussels, the only foundation made by Pierre-Julien Eymard outside of France, was able to serve as a refuge and a safeguard for the future.

A few years later a House was founded in Rome. But it was only towards the end of 1899 that the informative inquiries were begun, following the earnest entreaty of His Eminence Lucido Cardinal Parocchi, protector of the Congregation.

On April the 30th of that year hearings were opened at Paris at which there testified, in the city of Paris itself then at Belley and at

Angers, sixty-five witnesses. In the Ordinary Inquiry of Grenoble, begun on February 5, 1900, eighty-nine witnesses were heard, thirty-eight of whom were of the Diocese of Grenoble; the others were interviewed by tribunals established in the Dioceses of Fréjus, Toulon, Lyon and Rome.

The Reverend Edmond Tenaillon, Postulator of the Cause, had supervised the preparation and the functioning of these various processes with such persevering care, that by 1902 thirteen large volumes containing the findings of the Episcopal inquiries were ready for presentation to the Sacred Congregation of Rites, to be transcribed and serve as documents for the first discussion in the presence of the Cardinals.

On August 8, 1905, the decree concerning the revision of the writings of Pierre-Julien Eymard, was signed.

Finally, on August 12, 1908, the Order learned with great joy that the Sovereign Pontiff, taking in hand the cause of the Servant of God, had deigned to appoint a commission to introduce this Cause, and then, in accordance with the custom still prevailing at that time, Father Pierre-Julien Eymard had right to the title of Venerable.

Pope Pius X gave audience following September 23rd, to the members of the General Chapter, held at their House of St Claude. He closed his speech with these words: "I give my blessing to the Cause of your Venerable Founder, who was inspired by God in his work, because his glorification by the Universal Church, will be another approval given by Jesus Christ Himself to your rule and at the same time a strengthening of your vocation." The Blessing of the Vicar of Jesus Christ bore fruit. The letters of the Sacred Congregation of Rites, charging the Ordinaries of Grenoble and Paris, to make another investigation in the name of the Pope concerning the virtues of the Venerable Founder, were sent without further delay, and thanks to the indefatigable activity of Father Edmond Tenaillon, the Apostolic investigations proceeded in their course. In the meantime, on August 10, 1909, the Decree of *Super non Culta* was given. As early as December 5, 1910, the Postulator obtained from the Sacred Congregation of Rites, the order for the opening of the Apostolic Inquiry, but after having accomplished his work outside of Rome, a prodigious task, and assuring the fruits of his labors, he was called by death, on June 4, 1911. His name will always be associated with the Cause, which was carried on by him with so much zeal, because it is due to his untiring labor for more than twelve years, that the information was secured which made the Beatification possible.

The passing of the first Postulator did not hinder the progress of the Cause, as all the necessary documents were now in the possession of the Roman Curia. The Decree *De Fama sanctitatis* was published on April 9, 1913; and another called: *De validitate omnium processum,* on November 11, 1914. On April 30, 1918, the discussion regarding the heroism of the virtues of Venerable Pierre-Julien Eymard, was opened at the Ante-preparatory Congregation held by the Cardinal Ponent of the Cause, His Eminence Antonio Cardinal Vico, Pro-Prefect of the Sacred Congregation of Rites. The Preparatory Congregation took place on November 23, 1920, at the Vatican, in the presence of the Cardinals forming the Sacred Congregation of Rites, and the General Congregation took place on May 16, 1922, in the presence of His Holiness Pope Pius XI, who ordered the publication, on June 11, feast of the Blessed Trinity, of the Decree proclaiming the heroic virtues of Venerable Pierre-Julien Eymard.

As the Apostolic Inquiries had already been made concerning the two cures attributed to the intercession of Venerable Pierre-Julien Eymard, preparations were made at once for the discussion of the miracles. Four Doctors (two for each cure) received from the Sacred Congregation of Rites the commission to examine the facts, and their reports, duly sworn to, concluded that both cases were clearly supernatural.

The Ante-preparatory Congregation met in presence of the Cardinal Ponent on June 17, 1924. According to custom, two more doctors (one for each case) were appointed to make a new examination. As their reports were again in favor of the miraculous, the Preparatory Congregation was held at the Vatican, in the presence of the Cardinals composing the Sacred Congregation of Rites, on March 10, 1925, and on May 5, the General Congregation was held in the presence of the Holy Father, who, on May 9, graciously consented to the publication of the Decree approving the two miracles.

XVIII

THE TWO MIRACLES — THE BEATIFICATION

The two miracles submitted to the Sacred Congregation of Rites for examination, and then to the Holy See for approbation were:

1. The instantaneous and perfect cure at Santiago, Chile, on June 20, 1916, of Miss Lucinda Cifuentes, who was suffering from cancer of the stomach.

2. The cure, also instantaneous and perfect at Angers, France, on January 17, 1919, of Miss Renée Fouchereau, of tuberculosis of the bone involving the left knee joint.

※

The disease from which Miss Lucinda Cifuentes suffered was cancer of the stomach. "When called by the family for the first time," said Dr Pacheco, "I was asked to give my opinion in writing, and I stated that there was absolutely no doubt that it was cancer, and my diagnosis agreed with that of five other physicians.

"Cancer is very easily recognized during the last stages of the disease, moreover, during my twenty-seven years of practice, I have never seen a more complete case of carcinoma of the stomach. Miss Cifuentes suffered most excruciating pains. All remedies were useless; injections of morphine did not alleviate the pain. She had been visited by other physicians before me, and they had given her but a few months to live. When I first saw her she looked like a skeleton covered with tissue paper, and the symptoms were those of one in her last extremity."

When Miss Cifuentes realized that all remedies were ineffective, she had recourse to Venerable Pierre-Julien Eymard, promising to make an offering towards the expenses of his Beatification if he would cure her within fifteen days. Great was her assurance of obtaining her request; she placed a picture, together with a relic of the Servant of God, on her stomach, and when she was seized with even greater pain, she would exclaim: "Venerable Pierre-Julien Eymard must cure me!"

She was not aware of the nature of her disease; she only knew that she had stomach trouble which caused her terrible pain.

The improvement began on April 27, that is to say, from that date the disease began to diminish. The complete cure, with relative change in her appearance, took place on Sunday, April 30, on which day she was able to eat as heartily as before her illness; color returned to her cheeks, and she regained her strength within a few days so that she was able to resume the active life she had been accustomed to lead previous to her illness. The doctors declared that the cancer had disappeared.

※

Renée Fouchereau, fifteen years old, was a patient at the Hospital of Saint-Blaise in Angers, France, at the beginning of 1919. The doctors had stated that for about three years she had been suffering from tuberculosis in her left knee and that her condition was very serious.

Early in April 1916, they had put her leg in a plaster cast. This caused the patient great suffering, because the leg having bent up, the doctor was obliged to stretch it out in order to make it the same length as the other.

Despite injections, cauterizing and various other treatments, such as sun baths and electric baths, no improvement was obtained.

The young girl was then obliged to walk with two crutches, the left leg encased in the plaster cast, and she could not place the foot ever so lightly on the ground without suffering most intense pain.

"We began, on January 11, 1919," the patient testified, "a novena to Venerable Pierre-Julien Eymard. During the first six days of the novena I suffered intense pain in the knee, but what was my surprise, when on the seventh day, which was a Friday, all pain had disappeared! The doctor pressed hard upon the parts which had been most painful, and he too was greatly surprised at seeing that he no longer hurt me. He waited a few days and seeing that the pains did not return, he removed the plaster cast and allowed me to walk without crutches. After taking an x-ray, he stated that the knee was in perfect condition. Since then I have never felt any pain."

This cure was as perfect as it had been instantaneous, and more than five years later (May 26, 1924) the physician in charge was able to state: "The left knee is decidedly like the right one; its perimeter is one centimeter less than the other. It is not painful even when pressed upon. All its ligaments are flexible and its color and temperature are normal. All its movements have their full extension. It can truly be said that the joint of the left knee is cured."

After the publication of the Apostolic Decree, declaring the virtues of Venerable Pierre-Julien Eymard to have been heroic, and of the other approving the two miracles, there still remained a final Congregation called *de Tuto* (on whether it was *safe* to proceed), before the Holy Father could decide on the Beatification. This Congregation, at which the Cardinals and Consultors gave their affirmative vote, was held in the presence of His Holiness, on May 12, 1925.

On June 2, together with other Decrees relative to Beatifications also to be solemnized during the Holy Year, the Sovereign Pontiff caused to be read the one in which he declared that it was possible to proceed with all security to the Beatification of Venerable Pierre-Julien Eymard.

Only twenty-five years have passed—something certainly very

rare in the history of Beatifications—between the opening of the Informative Processes and the decision which placed the Servant of God on the Altars!

On July 12, at the close of the magnificent series of Canonizations and Beatifications of the Jubilee Year, there took place in the Basilica of St Peter, the solemn ceremony, during which, after the reading of the "Brief of Beatification" and the singing of the *Te Deum,* there was unveiled in the "Glory" the radiant image of him who from now on would be for our Holy Mother the Church:

Blessed PIERRE-JULIEN EYMARD.

About The Cenacle Press at Silverstream Priory

An apostolate of the Benedictine monastery of Silverstream Priory in Ireland, the mission of The Cenacle Press can be summed up in four words: *Quis ostendit nobis bona*—who will show us good things (Psalm 4:6)? In an age of confusion, ugliness, and sin, our aim is to show something of the Highest Good to every reader who picks up our books. More specifically, we believe that the treasury of the centuries-old Benedictine tradition and the beauty of holiness which has characterized so many of its followers through the ages has something beneficial, worthwhile, and encouraging in it for every believer.

cenaclepress.com

Also Available:

Robert Hugh Benson
The Friendship of Christ

Robert Hugh Benson
Confessions of a Convert

Fr Willie Doyle, SJ
Pamphlets for the Faithful

Dom Pius de Hemptinne, OSB
A Benedictine Soul: Biography, Letters, and Spiritual Writings of Dom Pius de Hemptinne

Blessed Columba Marmion, OSB
Christ the Ideal of the Monk

Blessed Columba Marmion, OSB
Words of Life on the Margin of the Missal

St John Henry Newman (*ed.* Melinda Nielsen)
Festivals of Faith: Sermons for the Liturgical Year

Fr Ryan T. Sliwa
New Nazareths in Us

Dom Hubert van Zeller, OSB
Approach to Prayer

Dom Hubert van Zeller, OSB
Sanctity in Other Words

Visit www.cenaclepress.com for our full catalogue.

www.ingramcontent.com/pod-product-compliance
Lightning Source LLC
Chambersburg PA
CBHW030307100526
44590CB00012B/546